Exes and Ohs

Exes and Ohs

A Downtown Girl's (Mostly Awkward) Tales of Love,

Lust, Revenge, and a Little Facebook Stalking

Shallon Lester

THREE RIVERS PRESS • NEW YORK

Published in the United States by Three Rivers Press, an imprint
of the Crown Publishing Group, a division of Random House, Inc.,
New York.
www.crownpublishing.com

Three Rivers Press and the Tugboat design are registered trademarks
of Random House, Inc.

Library of Congress Cataloging-in-Publication Data
Lester, Shallon.
A downtown girl's (mostly awkward) tales of love, lust, revenge, and a
little Facebook stalking / by Shallon Lester. — 1st. ed.
p. cm.
1. Lester, Shallon. 2. Dating (Social customs)—Humor. 3. New York
(N.Y.)—Humor. I. Title.
PS3612.E825Z46 2011
814.'.6—dc22
[B]   2010050268

ISBN 978-0-307-88511-1
eISBN 978-0-307-88512-8

Printed in the United States of America

Book design by Maria Elias
Cover design by Jessie Sayward Bright
Cover image by William King / Getty Images

10 9 8 7 6 5 4 3 2 1

First Edition

To Lt. Ryan James Adams, U.S. Army—
if I know what love is, it is because of you.

Contents

Introduction

"*Oh, Shallon, please,*" my agent said. "That did *not* happen." My editor said the same thing, as did my mom, grandmother, and friends. Even Owl, my kitten, meowed something along those lines.

But, friends, let me assure you that everything you are about to read in this book *is* in fact true. Unfortunately. I *wish* that these seventeen tales of love, loss, revenge, hockey, condoms, car thieves, hookers, Teenage Mutant Ninja Turtles, and many, many men were nothing more than fantasies. But alas, this really is my life, for better or for worse. A few names have been changed to protect the truly wicked, though they probably don't deserve such anonymity. Hopefully you'll enjoy these tales as much as my therapist has.

Non-Perishable

After one particularly heinous day as a gossip reporter, I stopped into my local bakery on the way home. I needed a cookie to cheer myself up.

The Romanian lady working behind the counter looked as bedraggled as I felt, and pretty soon we were swapping workplace horror stories as I stuffed my face with day-old scones and let her teach me Gypsy curses to mumble under my breath at work.

As she closed up shop, she offered me leftover bagels to take home, free.

"Ve just trow dem away, you should take instead," she said insistently, already stuffing baked goods into a paper bag. "You young girl, you need bread!"

I shrugged and accepted, figuring that between me and my three other roommates, Sarah (aka "Pfeiffer"), Marcia, and Holly, we could find some drunken use for a few bagels.

But she didn't give me a few. She gave me twenty. Twenty goddamn bagels. Even for the most ardent carbohydrate fan (me), that was a tall order. I stared at the bagels, starchy little enemies, as they taunted me, *begged me* to eat them all. They'd be rock-hard stale in less than a day; what in hell was I going to do with them—build a fort?

But I couldn't just trash them! In my family, being wasteful was a capital crime. My great-grandmother had survived the Depression and never missed an opportunity to remind us. In her house, ziplock bags were washed out and reused until they looked like a CDC experiment, and toothpaste tubes were cut in half to mine every last drop. You don't even want to know her thoughts on tampons.

Needless to say, tossing out food was just not an option. God help us if we ever made too many pancakes or anything else that didn't thrive well as a leftover. We sat at that table and ate until we were nauseous, because we'd rather punish our stomachs and arteries than wash any perfectly good grub down the drain.

Eventually, I found a better place for excess food than my strained tummy: the homeless.

I always had a very soft spot for the indigent. In the manicured suburbs of Orange County, we simply didn't have hobos. If one popped up, police would drive him outside city limits and drop him off in a more "poverty-friendly town," like Costa Mesa or Santa Ana. Something with a more Mexican-sounding name than "Irvine." For most of my town's residents, it was easy to forget that poor people even existed.

Not for me. Growing up with a single mom, I was all too familiar with life on an extreme budget. My grandmother and great-grandmother served as my babysitters and surrogate parents while my mama worked two jobs. Thanks to them, we were able to afford a nice house and bountiful Christmases, but I was lucky and I knew it.

So I began donating to charity in whatever way I could. When

I got old enough to drive I would scour our house to make care packages for the homeless. I raided the bathroom closet for pilfered hotel soaps and large, unwanted T-shirts from this 5K or that student council event. I'd cook up a Costco-sized box of macaroni and cheese and divide it into old margarine tubs, then write inspirational notes on napkins.

"You are loved!"

"Have faith, believe in yourself!"

"Fuck the police!"

I would leave the house with a trunk full of goodies, smugly optimistic about my goodwill mission. Inevitably, three pointless hours later, I'd be in tears.

Like I said, the homeless were in short supply in my area. Finding them was damn near impossible. I'd waste a whole tank of gas driving around random parks, hoping to find some sign of indigence. Once, in total desperation, I offered a care package to a woman who was very much *not* homeless, just sitting on a park bench sunning herself.

Lemme tell you something: the housed do not like being mistaken for the homeless. Not one little bit.

Even worse, I made this mistake a few times. I couldn't help it! Hoodies, dirty shoes, any sign of mumbling to oneself—these were *all* telltale homeless traits! How was I supposed to know that one guy had a Bluetooth in or that another chick was just having some sort of sexual identity crisis?

My mom found my gaffes hilarious, telling me I was cursed as I gagged down the wasted tubs of tepid mac and cheese all by myself.

Once I got to New York, though, the homeless were much easier to spot, and I went back to the handouts. As a waitress at Houston's, I was appalled at how much food was wasted. The steak house threw away hundreds of plump baked potatoes every night, so I began collecting them. I stuffed them clandestinely in my pockets and lurched out of the restaurant, hot taters slapping against my thighs as I waddled to the church steps where the hobos slept.

I can only imagine how terribly odd I must have looked to these poor people. A random blond girl, dressed all in black with an apron, like a side-dish ninja, producing potatoes out of a hidden pocket, then disappearing back into the night.

Of course, from then on, my crimes only escalated. It infuriated me that customers would take two bites of their massive rack of ribs and wave it away. So eventually, I started wrapping up leftovers and handing them out too.

Once, my fat bitch manager, Alexis, caught me. We hated each other, and she was probably delighted to confront me about pilfering food scraps.

"Shallon, this week we watched you steal ribs, spinach dips, half-eaten hamburgers, and part of a cobbler. Why?"

"I, I give them to the homeless," I peeped, knowing Alexis was picturing me gobbling up these germy bits of food in whatever hovel I lived in.

"Oh *please*," she snorted, "you do not."

She only believed me after I described my "route" in painful detail, but she still told me I had to stop because if something I fed them made them sick, they could sue Houston's. *Obviously* that was even more incentive to keep it up—I hated that restaurant and would've loved to have a poor person get rich off its back. I started including her business card with every potato.

But once I left that hellhole and got an office job, half-eaten chicken wings or any other leftovers were hard to come by. Until the day I met my Romanian Gypsy! As I stared at my booty of bagels, I felt the glorious thrill of charity—and revenge.

I grabbed a big canvas shopping bag and padded over to my local market, where I picked up vats of mustard, mayo, cheese, and sliced lunch meat.

Only I didn't exactly buy the meat . . .

I stole it.

I'd never stolen anything in my life. But then again, I'd never hated any grocery store chain more than this one. It was a ratty (literally—rodents were everywhere), overpriced cesspool, always full of the rudest employees available. One cashier called me a "white bitch" when I tried to return a carton of rotten milk.

Plus, I was a staunch vegetarian. I considered stealing meat a little "fuck you" to both the grimy store *and* the vile meat industry.

With that simple bag of free bagels, I became the Robin Hood of cold cuts.

My roommate Marcia came home that night to find sandwich fixins sprawled out all over the kitchen.

"So you're going back on meat . . . but . . . only cheap meat?" she guessed.

I told her giddily of my plan—make sandwiches and give them to the homeless!

"You *stole* the meat?!"

I laughed maniacally, my mayo-covered fists held high like a mad scientist, and I piled the sandwiches into my bike basket.

"This isn't a great idea, Shallon," said my other roommate Holly. "You're going to ride around the projects, alone, at night? You're going to end up as an episode of *Law & Order.*"

I considered the headline: BEAUTIFUL YOUNG DO-GOODER GUNNED

DOWN IN GHETTO—SATCHEL OF MEAT, INSPIRATIONAL NOTES FOUND ON BODY.

When I told my mom my plan, she didn't think I was going to have much luck either.

"Just one tip, honey," she said, biting back laughter. "Remember that just because someone's wearing last-season's ankle boots, it doesn't make them homeless."

LOLZ, Mom. LOLZ.

I pooh-poohed everyone's worries and set off for the dodgy end of Chelsea.

The first few people I gave sandwiches to were lucid and grateful, and then . . . the curse struck again.

Oh, I'd found homeless people all right, but they wanted precisely *nothing* to do with me and my sliced-meat delicacies.

One woman said she didn't like whole wheat bread (pardon me, your majesty!), while another lady, clearly a crackhead, was looking for more than a sandwich.

"You seen my boyfriend?" she said suspiciously, peering into my basket like I'd stuffed him betwixt the pastrami.

"Um . . . no, can't say I have," I mumbled, holding out food hesitantly.

And of course she had a boyfriend and I didn't. *Of course.*

"'Cause I ain't tryin' to let no sammich bitch take my man, you feel me, nigga?"

I put the food on a bench and backed away slowly as she eyed it, waiting for it to morph into Jamal or Big Skeezy, or whatever her Prince Charming was named.

And then there was the drunken gentleman who not only refused my sandwich . . . but offered *me* a dollar, his eyes full of pity.

But then I met Artie.

When I rode by, he was leaning on his cane outside of the market, asking politely for change. When people are begging for change, I'm always hesitant to offer them food, figuring they want cash for drugs or booze. Not that I blame them—that's what I spend most of my money on too.

But Artie was neither drunk nor high when he accepted my turkey on wheat. Instead, he was a charming, middle-aged black man from Mississippi, the kind who seemed like he wore bow ties and played the trumpet. Before I knew it, we were sitting on the curb chatting like old friends.

Artie told me that his girlfriend had just kicked him out again—why do the homeless date more than I do?—something she liked to do when his arthritis was acting up. He had two children down in Virginia who were trying to get him to move in with them, but for some reason he waved off the idea.

He asked me if I was a Christian, and I told him I wasn't but let him tell me about the Bible anyway. From that day on, whenever Artie was hanging outside the grocery store, I'd go in and get him a sandwich.

Make that *steal* him a sandwich.

It was a piece of cake, really. I'd go up to the deli counter and deal with the Jamaican woman who liked to pretend she didn't know what a sandwich was until I had to call the manager over. Then, once she had oh-so-graciously slapped a few slices of cheese and baloney on a roll, I'd simply slip the sammy in my purse the second I stepped into the next aisle.

The key to good thievery is twofold: 1) Defy stereotypes. In a neighborhood full of shady characters, no one is betting on the blond chick to be the criminal mastermind. 2) Always buy something. Trotting around a store for fifteen minutes and then leaving empty-handed raises suspicions. But if you walk out with a plastic bag, no one really cares what's in it.

Sometimes I'd buy—yes, *buy*—Artie new glasses, or, if it was Friday, a bottle of his favorite blackberry brandy.

I liked to think that in a way, I was his guardian angel, and I dreamed of getting a windfall of cash and using it to help him get off the streets. But then one day I saw him so drunk he could barely stand up. He had no clue who I was and hollered something in my direction that sounded suspiciously like "honkey."

I slunk away, embarrassed and hurt and depressed, and proceeded to do the only thing I know how to do when it comes to men who aren't appreciating me: make him jealous.

The next day I struck up a friendship with a street woman named Cheryl. I had seen her before, bloated and filthy, and figured that she was too mentally ill to approach. But that's the thing with the poor: they surprise you. She was actually perfectly normal, almost tragically so. I started bringing her full-on care packages—shoes, clothes, soaps, and deodorant—and in return she'd advise me on how to properly wrap my sprained ankle or where to find the best meatball sandwiches in Chelsea.

As she talked I would stare at the faded butterfly tattoo on her arm, and I imagined what her life was like when she got it done. Perhaps she was young and wide-eyed, getting her first ink at the behest of some shaggy-haired boyfriend she thought she'd marry one day.

I wondered when the tide of tragedy turned for Cheryl. I wondered when it turned for Artie, and for the lady searching for her boyfriend. I thought about my own lean bank account and recreational drug habit. Would it turn for me?

The answer came on a chilly Saturday morning in November. My roommates had gotten wasted the night before, but I'd stayed in on account of my seven A.M. hockey practice, so by eight thirty, when it wrapped up, I was bright eyed and wandering the streets with all my equipment.

Rock of Love wasn't on for another four hours, and the girls certainly weren't yet up to share their drunken tales. So, with my equipment and hockey stick in tow, I decided to pop into Gristedes and swipe some fixins for bacon-egg-and-cheeses; the church down the street that offered meals on weekdays to the homeless was tied up with its Baptist service, so there would be plenty of street people needing breakfast.

I lumbered into the store and immediately attracted attention— never a good thing—thanks to my gargantuan hockey bag and stick.

"The hell she got there?" the cashier, Tameka, sneered to the bag boy.

He shook his head. "I don't fuckin' know," he drawled, eyeing me with vague suspicion. "Prolly a body or sumthin'; you know how them white folks are."

In hindsight, I should have just paid for the goddamned eggs. But no. After weeks of thievery, I had grown cocky and brazen. I spent a solid ten minutes in the dairy aisle carefully wedging four dozen eggs into my hockey bag, cushioning them with several packages of bacon I'd stuffed in my skate slots.

I figured that due to the early hour, it wasn't busy enough for anyone to be patrolling the aisles looking for criminals. Well, I was half-right. They didn't need to patrol because, unbeknownst to me, my entire caper was committed in full view of the cashiers. The egg case was a straight shot from the checkout, and since there were no customers for Tameka to annoy and berate, she had plenty of time to watch me steal.

So when I came sauntering up to the register with a few bags of stale-looking croissants—and nothing else—Tameka was on high alert.

"Get all that shit out cho bag," she said, wagging her finger at my bulky Reebok duffel.

Of course, I played dumb. At this point, I had become such an adept thief, I was almost more comfortable lying than telling the truth.

"My equipment?" I blinked innocently.

"*No*," Tameka hollered, leaning over the Juicy Fruit display to thrust her pudgy, accusing finger at my bag. "Git them *eggs* out cho bag, bitch!"

"*Bitch?!*" I roared back. "Don't you *dare* call me a bitch, you trash!"

"Lionel!" Tameka turned around and hollered for the geriatric security guard.

Out of the corner of my eye, I noticed that a small crowd had formed outside the nearby exit. A few of the neighborhood people who regularly loitered in front of the store were craning their necks to get a better view of the ruckus.

Lionel, not at all pleased at having to put down his copy of the *Post*, came shuffling over.

"Girl, what's all this about right here?" he grumbled.

"I am trying to pay for these croissants and she just called me a bitch!"

"First of all," Tameka shrieked, "you *are* a bitch, and you a stealin' bitch, too!"

She wheeled toward Lionel.

"She got a whole messa *eggs* in that big ol' weird sack, you just go on an' look!"

With the gait of a man long accustomed to being screeched at by women, Lionel started toward my hockey bag.

I was cornered.

I instinctively tensed up and crouched as I seized my stick for protection. I was fully prepared to fight my way out of there. Tameka and Lionel were looking at the business end of a hissy fit. That was one unexpected upshot to my hockey hobby—I would punch a bitch anytime, anywhere, with zero forethought or regrets. I briefly considered whether I had enough time to snatch my skates out, shove my hands inside them, and windmill out the door, flying fists of razor-sharp fury.

No, I decided, *the stick is easier to maneuver.*

Suddenly, everything seemed to happen at once; Lionel moved in, Tameka bellowed "Biiiiitch!" one last time, and I'm pretty sure I bared my teeth and hissed. Then, as the tussle for the eggs ensued, a dark flash streaked into the room!

"You *git off her, damn it!*"

It was Artie, half-drunk and wild-eyed, brandishing a large glass object in each hand.

"Artie! What are you—"

"Jus' run, *run, girl!*" He paused briefly to confront Lionel and Tameka, and I finally identified his weapons of choice: two empty bottles of blackberry brandy. *"Run!"*

I finally snapped into action and started to hustle past him and out of the store. Lionel and Tameka were useless to stop me. They were either too scared or too confused.

But as soon as I was past them, Lionel lunged for Artie, who began swinging the bottles wildly. What ensued was less of an actual beat-down and more of a tween-girl slap fight. Both men were shrieking like bats, and in the heat of battle, Artie dropped the bottles onto my hockey bag. There was a sickening thud, and I heard the eggs crack, but better the eggs than our skulls. I grabbed Artie by the collar and bolted.

I still don't know how I did it, but I managed to get my bag, stick, forty-eight oozing eggs, bacon, *and* a homeless man out of the store in one fell swoop.

"That was the most fun I've had in four years, I tell you what!" Artie laughed, panting, as we lurched around the corner. "That brandy sho did come in handy, now, eh?"

"Man, Artie, I never thought I'd be so glad to see a drunk!"

We laughed and I gave him a twenty-dollar bill.

"Ohh no," he said, "I didn't do that for money. I did that because you're like my guardian angel. And I was happy to be one for you!"

"Listen," I told him, "twenty bucks is a lot less than bail money, so just take it."

He grinned his toothless smile, like a wizened old baby, and reluctantly took the money. I headed home, leaving a gooey trail of egg matter behind me.

It took me an hour to get my equipment clean. Turns out, hot water essentially cooks raw eggs, and let me tell you, runny scrambled eggs aren't easy to get off elbow pads and Velcro.

I scrubbed and cursed, realizing that karma had at last caught up to my less-than-legal charity. I could take solace only in the fact that my slate had been wiped clean.

But no. It hadn't. The egg debacle was just a preview.

Eight days later, I was in the locker room suiting up for my team's playoff game.

"What in hell is that *smell*?" said our left-winger. "Jesus, does anyone else smell that?"

Clearly, we were used to a wide palette of scents in a hockey locker room.

"It's the stench of victory!" announced our massive goalie.

"Urrrgh, the heck it is," said our coach, gagging. "Something's gone rotten. That's what that is."

I felt a sweaty dread creep across the back of my neck. I recalled a line from one of my favorite movies, *Inside Man*, starring Clive Owen as a bank robber.

"The thing about evil deeds," he said in the film, "is that you can't cover them up. They *stink*."

The bacon.

In the end, on the downside, I had to pay $120 to have all my equipment dry-cleaned and disinfected—twice. On the upside, we won that playoff game. Turns out no one wants to body-check the girl who smells like rotted pork.

Giant Douche Rides Again

When I moved to New York, people had all sorts of advice about staying safe. Keep your money in a waist belt, avoid the subway after sundown, don't trust redheads—the usual.

But I wasn't worried about criminals or gingers. There was just one thing I feared above all else: running into my ex, Giant Douche. I had met him before I moved to the city and our romance started out great but quickly soured due to my being overly awesome and his being—hence the name—a giant douche. How giant? He did the Blow Job Head-Push on our first date and later would rate my looks on a scale of one to ten in front of his friends.

Worst of all, he was incredibly successful and I was incredibly a waitress. An incredibly bad waitress. I was not, how you say, "born to serve" or "be obedient in any way," so I loathed every single second of my tenure at the ninth circle of hell otherwise known as Houston's midtown restaurant.

So you can imagine my delight when one day, in the middle of the lunch shift and wearing my Houston's finest—clogs, a starched oxford, and black polyester pants that made me look like a highway patrolman—I rounded a corner and locked eyes with none other than Giant Douche. The eye contact lasted only a millisecond but I was sure I'd been caught, seen, exposed! For *six months* I had trotted around this city always just a swipe of gloss away from fabulousness, ready and willing to see him for the first time since our split, and now I was going to run into him while wearing a hairnet? The injustice of it just about killed me.

As much as I didn't want to see him ever again, I had foolishly believed that when I eventually did (after all, New York wasn't big enough for the two of us), I would be ready, no matter when or where it happened. Coming out of the gym? Fine. Mid–walk of shame? Fine. At the abortion clinic? *Fine.*

Anyplace but at Houston's, with me not only wearing an apron, but one covered with mayonnaise debris.

Luckily, I had had enough foresight to craft a shaky Giant Douche Contingency Plan in the event of this very catastrophe; I had made my work BFF Hilary swear to hit me in the head with a pan if he were ever to come in. That way I'd have an excuse to stay off the floor (and if I was lucky, unconscious) until he left. But the night it happened it wasn't her regular shift, and I was alone. No friends in sight. So I did what any rational person would do. I gave a new server five dollars to watch my tables, burrowed behind the potatoes in the storage closet, and hid.

"Giiiiirl, what's going on?" Gay James asked me.

"My ex!" I hissed through the iced tea filters. "He's at table twenty-four!"

"Oh, honey, no he ain't. You ain't been datin' a hot, gangly mess like *that*. No, no, no, child. Gay James is not believin' that for a second!"

What's worse, GD was with *a date*, a chubby blonde too plain to even be considered ugly. But he looked happy and healthy and good and the way I'd remembered him in the few pleasant memories of our relationship.

I called my friend Julie, hysterical.

"He's here at work! And he's with a *date!*" I shrieked, hunching down lower into my potato fort.

"He's on a date at your office?" she said, forgetting that I was still a minimum-wage peon. "Well, you should just go say hi and get it over with."

Say hi? Absolutely not, no, false. I would've ended up just vomiting, or nervously admitting I'd slept with his roommate (twice) after we'd broken up. "Seriously, Shall," Julie lied, "it could be worse."

Oh, could it? I would have rather run into him at the drugstore while trying to buy Anusol ointment with food stamps. Or perhaps on my way to a KKK rally. Or maybe fighting with a dog over a piece of pizza I found on the ground.

So I stayed hidden and skulked around the kitchen until my vile manager, Alexis, found me and forced me to take a spoon out to one of my tables. I slunk out, hugging the walls like a rat in a maze, and I fought the instinct to jab the spoon into my eye. My face burned with shame, and I was painfully aware that I was wearing clogs and smelled like bacon. *Greasy bacon.*

Maybe a Texan would've found that alluring, but Giant Douche was Jewish and found nothing charming about a pork-scented woman.

By some miracle, I managed to slither around the restaurant undetected until he left, and once the Xanax a kind colleague had given me to crush up in my iced tea kicked in, I breathed a sigh of relief.

But then, of course, I stupidly decided to blog about the incident. Only about twenty of my friends read Cherchez La Shallon, none of whom knew GD, so I thought it was safe to detail every ounce of my shame in my little corner of the Internet. But I didn't have the foresight to realize that the blog was the first thing to pop up on my Google results, which of course he found and called me out on.

You should have said hi . . . was the subject line of his e-mail, with a link to my blog post. Searing with embarrassment, I considered several options: A) hang myself with my hideous green apron, B) ignore the e-mail and pretend like the whole thing never happened, or C) invite him to meet for coffee, sometime when I was clean and normally scented, and bury the hatchet—i.e., show him that despite all evidence to the contrary, I was still hot and fabulous. A better person than I would have chosen C, of course. And I almost did. But I realized that I could wash my hands all I wanted with as much anti-bacon soap as I could find and it wouldn't do any good; the stench of desperation and shame tends to linger.

Hits and Missus

"*Are you going* to take me into the woods and kill me, Max?" I inched cautiously toward the Lamborghini. "Because if you are, I'm not getting in the car."

He slung an arm over the white leather headrest and smirked with amusement.

"Sweethawt," he drawled in his thick New York accent, "just get in the fuckin' cah."

This isn't how most third dates begin, I'm aware of that. But Max was no ordinary guy.

We met during one of my mind-numbing shifts at Houston's. I was aimlessly drifting around the dining room, massively hungover from my fifth straight night of partying until four A.M., when a short, wiry guy in a bespoke suit came sauntering up to me.

"Honey, I have a problem," he said, twisting his platinum cuff-links in a way that implied power, not anxiety. He was short yet confident and looked a lot like Stanley Tucci. I wasn't impressed.

"The bathroom is that way." I sighed and turned to walk away, but he caught my arm. He was stronger than he looked.

"Nah, I don't need the bathroom, honey," he said. "The problem is, I'm in love with you."

I bit back a chuckle and looked around to see if someone was playing a prank on me.

"I am," he said, looking me dead in the eye, which, as a waitress accustomed to serving drunk tourists, was not something I was used to. "I'm in love with you, and I'm taking you to dinner this week."

I blinked dully for a few minutes. Who was this guy? He was small, bald, had a slight lisp, and yet . . . there was something alluring about him, a dynamism that settled over you like a hypnotic blanket.

"Dinner?" I said thickly.

"Yeah, I wanna take you to Nobu this Thursday. You ever been to Nobu before?"

I was a celebrity in my own mind, so yes, I'd dined there many times with Jay-Z and Beyoncé, maybe an occasional brunch with Rob De Niro or dessert with Taylor Swift. But in the real world, I instead spent my evenings prowling around the Meatpacking District with Klo, boozing it up at douche castles like Marquee and Level V. We knew every doorman in Manhattan and would stay out all night no matter what the temperature or what time the alarm was going off, which didn't leave a whole lot of time for fine dining.

But the scene was starting to get a little old. If you've met one smarmy promoter or washed-up model, you've met them all. So before I could think of a viable reason to turn him down, I found myself accepting his offer and exchanging numbers.

"So should I just meet you there?" I asked. I couldn't really remember how dates worked; it had been ages since I'd been on a real, proper one that didn't start and end on the dance floor at an after-hours club.

"Nah, nah, I'll come pick you up," he said, waving off the idea. "Where you live, SoHo? You seem like a stylish, downtown kinda girl."

Most people wouldn't expect a waitress in a midtown steakhouse to make enough money to live in the most sought-after neighborhood in Manhattan. Lucky for me, I didn't require things like elevators, working heaters, or bedrooms that could fit two people at the same time, and thus I was able to afford a room in a sixth-floor walk-up off Mott Street.

That Thursday, Max rolled up to my apartment in a $100,000, black-on-black, S-Class Mercedes convertible. He was dressed immaculately in another custom-made suit—gray, with a pink shirt and lavender tie—and held my door open as I slid into the soft leather seats.

"Um . . . what do you do for a living?"

He smiled inwardly as the engine purred to life. "Cupcakes," he said. "I own a cupcake store in Brooklyn. Sunshine Bakery."

"Cupcakes," I repeated flatly, trying to figure out how owning a bakery that I'd never heard of afforded him a car worth more than most Mississippi real estate. The truth was, I didn't really care. He was rich, charming, and flashy. And considering I served prime rib for a living and wasn't really in the position to be picky, that was enough.

"I'll take you there sometime," he said. "I'll even name a new cupcake after you, how'd that be?"

I giggled like a piglet, so easily flattered. I couldn't picture what a Shallon confection might taste like. Oooh, maybe a peanut butter cupcake with a razor blade inside! We could call it Sweet Revenge!

I quickly made a mental list of people I'd love to give a Sweet Revenge to, before snapping back into reality. I still wanted some basic info on this guy.

"So where are you from, anyway?"

"France."

He said his last name was LeCavalier, but he didn't look French at all; he looked Italian. But whatever, America's the melting pot, blah blah blah—did I mention the $100,000 car? As we pulled up to the restaurant, he reached across my lap to lock the glove box, and I saw what looked like the edge of a tattoo peeking out of his collar.

"Do you have a tattoo on your back?"

"Umm . . . no," he said, "not really."

"Not really? It's kind of a yes-or-no question, Max."

He leaned over, caressed my cheek softly with his hand, and said, "You're beautiful, you know that?"

Tattoo what? Who? Huh? I melted like a sack of sugar left out in the rain. I'm such a sucker for a sweet talker.

Dinner was delicious and lavish, and he asked me endless questions about myself, but not in an interrogative way, like most guys. He actually seemed to be *listening* and interested. I realize now that he was merely trying to deflect attention away from himself, but at the time his mystery only made me like him more.

After dinner he suggested dessert at a rice pudding joint by my house. Now, the concept of rice pudding is very foreign to West Coasters. Rice and pudding were never two things any Californian had considered combining; we're a fro-yo sort of people. But I didn't want to look provincial so I agreed to give it a go.

He ordered me a cup of chocolate vomit (I mean rice pudding) as I got us a table. He seemed to know the manager and didn't even bother trying to pay.

"Here you go, doll-face," Max said, kissing me on the cheek and plopping a bowl of mucus-like "dessert" in front of me. "I need to go take care of something, stay here."

In a flash he had disappeared through the employees-only door, leaving me to poke at the gelatinous mass. I figured he'd gone to the bathroom, but a few moments later he reappeared, tucking something into his breast pocket and looking slightly agitated.

"Let's go," he snapped, grabbing me firmly but gently by the elbow.

"But don't you want to try my snot pile—"

He leveled his gaze. "I said, let's *go.*"

It wasn't exactly threatening, but something told me not to argue. Bewildered, but thankful to escape the disgusting rice pudding, I trotted out to the Benz. We swooped around the corner to a pizza parlor and he parked out front. But as I started to get out, he told me to stay put.

"I just need to run an errand," he said. "Stay in the fucking car—don't let *anyone* touch the car."

I had no problem sitting there like a princess, imagining that I was a rich housewife and very much accustomed to hanging out in jillion-dollar automobiles.

A few minutes later Max came ambling back out, taking yet another envelope out of his pocket and locking it in the glove box.

Before I knew it we were in front of my apartment, and he leaned in confidently for a kiss. I really wasn't that attracted to him, but I didn't have anyone better to kiss at the moment, so I let him. He didn't try to push for more than a PG-13 smooch, which struck me as very strange indeed. Men in New York expect a visit to third base if they so much as buy you a Bud Light, never mind a $200 dinner. But Max had an oddly patient quality and it was refreshing.

I agreed to meet him the following week for supper at Fiamma, another fabulously expensive restaurant I had no hope of affording on my own.

"I've never heard of his cupcake shop," said Pfeiffer, my roommate and fellow pastryophile, as she trolled the Internet looking for Sunshine Bakery.

"Whatever." I shrugged. "I don't really care." But I had to admit, there *was* something off about Max, something he seemed to be hiding. Part of me wanted to get to the bottom of it, but the lazier, more dominant part of me was excited for another splashy night out.

The next Monday, after spending an hour tarting myself up, I stood patiently outside my apartment waiting for Max to pick me up.

Ten minutes.

Thirty minutes.

Forty-five minutes.

Nothing. I called him five times, leaving messages that progressed from curious to seething. I'd been waiting out there nearly an hour and the neighbors were starting to think I was a prostitute. Was this guy *seriously* standing me up?

Furious and blinking back tears, I tromped back to my apartment and straight to the refrigerator, where I self-medicated with Velveeta and *The Golden Girls* for the next two hours, weeping indignantly. I didn't even really like him and *he* was ditching *me*? Is this really what my life in this city had become? A few hours later, bloated from *queso* and crying, Max called.

I didn't answer. He called again. And again. And again—eleven times. Finally, I picked up the phone.

"Baby, I am *so sorry*," he gushed. "I got caught up in stuff at the store and I just couldn't get away—"

I interrupted with a tirade about how cell phones usually get reception inside bakeries and blathered about how humiliating it was to stand outside for hours (he deserved a little exaggeration).

"I know, you're right, I'm an asshole. I'm horrible. I'm the worst guy ever," he burbled. At least he wasn't even trying to defend himself. I liked that in a man. "Listen, lemme make it up to you tomorrow, okay? We'll have dinner at Per Se and then we can get a table wherever you want—Bungalow 8, Butter, wherever."

I looked around at my life—congealed cheese on the coffee table as Dorothy and Blanche bantered in the background—and realized that Max was making me a very decent offer. I agreed to see him the next night and vowed to make him wait twenty minutes before I deigned to come downstairs.

And when I did, there was Max sitting in not the Benz, but a yellow Ferrari. A Novitec F430 Bi-Compressor Evoluzione, to be exact. I didn't even know how to get into the damn thing; it looked like a Transformer. With a price tag so high it's not even advertised, it made the Benz look like a van with a tiger airbrushed on the side.

"All right, listen," I said sternly as I wedged myself inside the slipper of a car. "I find it really hard to believe that you can afford this . . . *machine* on a baker's salary. There's something you're not telling me."

Max sighed, like he knew this was coming. "C'mon, let's go for a drive."

We raced along the West Side Highway and he squeezed my hand tightly.

"You're right; I do need to tell you something." He chewed his lip pensively. "I . . . I kinda have . . . a wife."

"A *what*?" That was not what I was expecting to hear.

"I mean technically we're still married but we're separated."

"Are you *legally* separated?" I yanked my hand out of his.

"Well . . . not yet. But it's in the works. We're getting a divorce, honey."

I was vaguely aware that this confession did nothing to explain how he could afford these cars but I was shocked enough to be temporarily distracted, which I'm sure was his very goal.

"Does she know you've been seeing me?"

"Yes," he lied, his voice rising an octave. Men are so bad at this. "I told her all about you."

I rolled my eyes and shook my head. Truth was, I've never been an overly moral person and a wife was his problem, not mine. I even sort of appreciated the fact that he was motivated enough to be unfaithful. But you can't just shrug and say "NBD!" To be ladylike you must at least *pretend* to care.

"I just can't believe this, Max," I huffed. "First you stand me up and now I find out that you're breaking your sacred covenant of marriage!"

WTF was I talking about? The righteous and ethical were so foreign to me, I didn't even know what vocabulary they used.

I pouted and feigned iciness for a few more minutes before oh-so-reluctantly agreeing to still have dinner with him. Seven courses later he was dropping me off again. I had given in and enjoyed the thousand-dollar dinner but was too tired and full to partake in a boozy night out at a club. I permitted him one French-less kiss as he dropped me off, just to punish him for being such a jerk. At least that was my excuse, anyway. This was kind of an interesting experiment—me masquerading as a chaste, virtuous little girl in the city. I was ready to be done with the debauched phase required of every new Manhattanite, I reasoned, and maybe Max could save me from myself. I realize that a cheating husband is not the ideal shepherd to a life of morality, but hey, beggars couldn't be choosers.

Truthfully, though, the Ick was beginning to set in. You know the Ick: it's the skin-crawlingly disgusted feeling you get when you're not attracted to a guy. It's not reserved for ugly people—I've had the Ick for perfectly handsome, hygienic guys. But for some reason, I wanted nothing to do with them sexually. Maybe they were too nice or too fawning, but whatever the reason, eventually I'd be shivering with revulsion if they even tried to hold my hand. You can't help the Ick—it's an uncontrollable response, a terminal cancer on a relationship. Once the Ick sets up shop, it's there forever. The smart move is to just cut off the romance, like a gangrenous limb. Try to deny it and it'll eat you alive.

But then again, Max wasn't making any demands on me sexually, and he actually seemed to *like* my sassiness. So I let him make plans for us to see *La Bohème* at the Met the next Friday. It would be our third date, and from what *Cosmo* says, that's when you're supposed to explore his "bod" and "moan zones." I didn't think Max was expecting to go from good-night kisses to shagging, but men don't make sense. We know this. So just to be on the safe side, I prepared a long list of sexually deterrent excuses as I got ready that night.

It's that time of the month.

I'm worried my parents will find out.

I'm nervous that your wife gave you AIDS—let's swing by the clinic on the way home.

I respect you too much to ever want to see you naked. Ever.

Turns out, he would be the one making excuses. That night I waited outside, again, this time for thirty minutes before I realized that Max wasn't coming. Part of me was relieved; I didn't even bother leaving him an enraged voice mail. There was something very shady about this guy; the wife, the oddly lucrative business, the tattoo. Was he with his wife? Had she found out? Pfft, found out *what*? That we'd been to dinner and kissed like sixth-graders? Big whoop.

I took off my fancy dress, cut a block of Velveeta from the log, and plopped on the couch. A few minutes later, my phone rang. An automated voice greeted me.

"This is the New York City police department, First Precinct. Will you accept a collect. Call from. *Max Borgia*."

Who the hell was Max Borgia?

"I'm the worst, I'm horrible, honey, I'm so sorry."

"I—what? Where are you? Why are you calling me collect?"

He took a deep breath. "I'm in jail."

"*Jail?*" Surely this was a joke. Maybe Jail was a cool new lounge I hadn't heard of.

"Yeah. I'm so sorry, doll-face, I've been with the DA for the last few hours, they just now let me use the phone."

"Jail," I repeated thickly, still trying to understand how my love life had morphed into an episode of *Law & Order*.

"Listen, I'm leaving here soon, I'm coming over and picking you up."

"What? No!" I shrieked. "No no no! I don't know what kind of trouble you're in but I don't want any part of it, Max. I don't even know your last name!"

"Shallon, listen," he said gravely, his voice dropping into a low rumble. "I need to explain some things. I'm not who you think I am."

A chill ran up my spine, but I was too curious to hang up on him. An hour later he was outside my house, immaculately dressed, as always, with his arm slung over the headrest, coaxing me into a Lamborghini Murcielago—a third car, for, technically, our third date.

"C'mon, honey, I'm not gonna kill you." He patted the ostrich-leather seat invitingly. "C'mon, where you wanna go?"

"Someplace with witnesses," I mumbled nervously, and gingerly climbed in.

We drove to the Spotted Pig and nestled into a corner table. Max quickly ordered us both whiskeys. Up until now he'd been strictly a champagne man, so I knew whatever he had to tell me wasn't good if he needed a Johnnie Walker buffer.

He took a deep swig of liquor and began.

"First of all, let me start with things that *are* true. I *do* own a cupcake store, but that's not how I make my money. I *am* separated from my wife, but no, we're not divorced. And my name *is* Max, but not LeCavalier. I'm not French."

I wrinkled my nose, totally confused. "I—you're not—but then if you don't . . . ?"

I had no idea how to even begin responding. He took my hand gently, patiently, and began to unravel the long yarn of lies he'd spun over the past month.

"You know why I have so many cars? Because I steal them. Long story short, I run a ring of car thieves and basically, that's what I got pinched for tonight. I wouldn't be telling you any of this if the feds didn't already know, so don't worry that you're keeping secrets for me or anything."

My head was swimming. I pictured Max as the Artful Dodger to a ragtag gang of street urchins with names like Little Tony and Spitball. Under Max's orders, they would slim-jim their way into cars and, as payment, were allowed to keep whatever change or gum they found inside. But for some reason the life of crime wasn't what immediately bothered me.

"We've been driving around in someone else's car?!" I yelped, suddenly getting a massive case of the creeps. "Oh my *God*, Max, *gross*!"

He rolled his eyes. "Honey, we weren't using their fuckin' toothbrush, okay? And these cars haven't belonged to anyone yet—we got 'em off the boat. Anyway, I use a French last name because it puts a little distance between me and the people I'm . . . *connected* to."

I realized that my vision of Max and his merry band of orphans was an underestimation of his talent. He wasn't some half-assed street thug—Max was in the Mafia.

I hadn't lived in New York for very long, but I was already becoming very accustomed to unpleasant dating surprises. Oh, you're actually nineteen and live in the dorms? Great. That girl isn't your sister but your live-in girlfriend? Marvelous. The jar of powdered sugar in your kitchen is really cocaine? Faaaantastic.

Along the way, I'd learned to desensitize myself to those sorts of mid-range lies. But Max's fictitious life was in a whole separate category.

I shook my head disbelievingly and tried to choke out a few basic questions.

"Did . . . did you get that tattoo in prison?"

He laughed, his sudden joviality startling me. "No, no, this took months to complete, it's not something some fuckin' jerk-off could do in the joint."

He turned his back to me and with one swift movement pulled up his shirt, exposing his entire illustrated back—a massive, multicolored portrait of the Pietà. The blessed virgin wept over his shoulder blades as her limp son's arms dangled to his waist. At her feet was etched an elaborate Latin phrase, but before I could try to decipher it he pulled his shirt back down and turned to face me, waiting patiently for more questions.

"So, they caught you," I asked, hoping that saying it aloud would help it make sense, "and now what? I mean, they let you go—that's a good thing, right?"

He smiled bitterly. "Nah, they didn't just turn me loose; I made bail. But I gotta report back next week to start my sentence."

"Your what?" My dodgy knowledge of the legal system was based entirely on what District Attorney Jack McCoy had taught me, but I was sure that Max was at least entitled to a trial. "Aren't you going to fight it?"

"Nah, baby," he said, squeezing my hand. "They got too much on me, and besides, they're only giving me a year—I take my chances at trial and I could get fifteen. Juries don't have warm and fuzzy feelings for the kind of people I do business with."

Suddenly I felt the hot sting of tears welling up in my eyes.

"You're going to prison? To *prison*?" It's not like I was in love with Max, but the thought of him being cooped up in a cell for an entire *year* was horrifying—he was so vivacious and dapper, so refined and dynamic! Would he come out bitter and twisted, with a teardrop tattoo on his face like Lil Wayne? Actual tears spilled onto my cheeks, and I found myself sobbing into my whiskey as a waitress discreetly slid me a napkin.

"Aw, baby, don't cry, please don't cry," he said, starting to panic the way all men do at the sight of female tears. "A year ain't nothin', really."

"But, how did they know?" I snuffled. "How did they catch you?"

Max stared out the window, his vivid eyes narrowing menacingly. "Someone ratted me out."

I value loyalty above anything else and it turned my stomach to think that someone sold Max down the river.

"Who?" I hissed. "*Who?*"

"Oh, I know who did it," he murmured, still gazing out the

window with a reptilian look in his eye. "I wouldn't worry about them anymore . . ."

I shivered, realizing that whoever was stupid enough to betray Max LeCavalier/Borgia was sure to meet a sticky, sticky end.

Good, I thought cruelly, *I hope he got two taps to the head and was left in a ditch somewhere. I hope it was slow and painful and—* I caught myself, shocked by my own maliciousness. Is this what I was becoming, a Mafia mistress wishing death on anyone who dared cross her boyfriend?

They say you're only as good as the company you keep. Suddenly, as I assessed my current compatriots—down-and-out waiters, club kids, coked-out models, alcoholic bankers, and now, a Mafioso—I realized that Max's appeal was not one of novelty. No no. It was one of *familiarity.* I had tried to pretend that his lifestyle—shady dealings with slimy people—was oh-so-foreign to me. It wasn't. He was simply a Technicolor version of myself—flashier, sneakier, more illegal—and I'd known it from the beginning; I just didn't want to admit it to myself.

I realized that I wasn't crying for him but for me; if I didn't cowboy the hell up, cut back the partying, and get out of Houston's, I'd find myself down a similarly dead-end path.

I'd been putting off applying for an assistant editor position at *FHM* a friend had told me about, but the Max episode now awoke a long-dormant sense of purpose within me, a feeling that had been lulled to sleep with vodka sodas and Britney Spears remixes. But enough was enough.

"Look, honey, I don't expect you to wait for me or nothin'," he said, "I just wanted to explain and, ya know, maybe after I get out I'll look you up and we can pick up where we left off."

It was the most respectful breakup I'd had in months. Maybe

ever. I nodded and kissed him good-bye, and hopped a cab home. The next morning I sent in my résumé to *FHM,* and a month later, I was throwing out my Houston's apron and settling into my new office.

I never did hear from Max again, but every time I read about a body being discovered in a shallow grave outside of Newark, I think of him, and I smile.

Bursts Under Pressure

"*Jesus Christ, how* many of these things do you have?!"

That's never something you want to hear your boyfriend say. Whether he's talking about cats, Girl Scout cookies, or body parts, it ain't a compliment. But my problem wasn't felines or Thin Mints. It was condoms.

Like most girls, the majority of my experiences with condoms were fraught with awkwardness and embarrassment, but not for the usual reasons. My problem isn't ineptitude or shyness; quite the opposite, actually. The issue is that I have so very many of them.

Hundreds.

Thousands.

Enough rubbers to supply a whorehouse at a Russian naval port until the end of time. Why? That's a good question, one that every paramour asks sooner or later.

"Well," I say sheepishly, suddenly very aware of my nakedness. "I'm sort of sponsored by Trojan."

"I'm sorry," the boy will say, "did you say you're *sponsored* . . . by a *condom company*?"

Visions of gangbangs and key parties swim in his head as he reels, grabbing the bedpost for support.

"No, no!" I exclaim in protest. "It's not like you think! I host parties for them and they just send me all these as a thank-you!"

Their next sentence is usually something along the lines of:

"What in hell does a condom party consist of, Shallon?"

At this point I have approximately forty-five seconds to explain how I got involved with Trojan, what I do for them, and why that equals the 2,350 condoms stuffed under my bed before their pants are back on and they're fleeing out the door.

The whole prophylactic saga began years ago, when I was an associate editor at *FHM* magazine. I was lucky enough to get the plum assignment of interviewing a scientist who worked for Trojan, nicknamed "Dr. Condom." Yes, he was the guy in charge of testing how well the rubbers worked and coming up with new, innovative ideas for how to keep gonorrhea—and lost erections—at bay.

My boss wanted me to get lots of pervy little sound bites from Dr. Condom about how he watches people have sex for a living. But I, the nerd-slut hybrid that I am, instead spent the interview grilling the scientist on which type of rubber would best suit my boyfriend Raylan.

Here's what I learned: Unless he's really small, pretty much every guy can wear Magnums. The only difference between them and regular condoms is that Magnums are wider at the base. This makes for a much more comfortable fit, allowing more blood to flow, which makes him harder, longer. Magnum XLs, on the other hand, are best left to professional athletes and porn stars; they're wider throughout and could probably cover a Volkswagen Beetle if necessary. That answered my questions about fit, but what about all the other typical dude objections? The key, the doc said, is to put a few drops of lube *inside* the condom—much more enjoyable for the guy.

I soaked up the information, even taking notes to show Ray later. He'd been complaining about condoms being too small—seriously, do guys still think that line works? We've all seen the health class demo where our teacher puts one over his head and inflates it by exhaling through his nose to show that any guy who claims "I'm just too big for them, baby" is full of crap—so now I had a viable solution. Magnums!

I ran out of work that day and straight to the drugstore, flying out with a shiny new box of rubbers I couldn't wait to test out.

The next day, a *very* satisfied Raylan texted me that he felt liberated by the Magnum experience, and my response will live in text-message infamy among my friends forever:

"*You are emancipated!*" I wrote back. "*And all thanks to me, the Abe Lincoln of sex!*"

"You wrote *what*?" said my best friend, Klo, not even trying to hide her horror.

"I . . . I thought it was funny," I said defensively. "Because he freed the slaves, you know? Like I freed his . . . never mind." I instantly regretted sending the SMS.

"Did he write back?"

"Well . . . not yet." I chewed my lip nervously.

I was always doing weird things like this that *I* thought were hilarious but ended up creeping out my boyfriends. You'd think that most boys would be so happy to have a fun, cool girlfriend they had great sex with that they would overlook the *occasional* Civil War–themed text. *Big deal.* But apparently it, or some other phantom flaw, *was* a big deal, because he broke up with me two weeks later. Even worse, it was the same day that a crate—yes, a crate—of Magnums was shipped to my office as a thank-you for the glowing Trojan article.

I am 1) probably the only girl who ever got a giant shipment of giant rubbers delivered to her work, and 2) certainly the only one ever to burst into tears upon receiving them. The boys in the office, however, were delighted and dove right into the pile, stuffing a box or two into their messenger bags as they fought over the ten Trojan vibe rings. But at the end of the day, I still had hundreds of Magnums left, all for me—and me alone. There were so many, I had to take a taxi home; I couldn't even carry them on my own. As I sat on my bed, surrounded by hundreds of shiny gold Magnum wrappers gleaming in the summer twilight, I felt like Scrooge McDuck with his money bin. Maybe I could fill the tub with them and splash around happily, reveling in a latex fortune. Instead, I stuffed them into an old duffel bag and exiled them to a dark corner under the bed.

Cut to two years later. I had started video-blogging for a men's advice site called Doubleagent.com. It was basically a site for dudes who wanted insight into the female mind, and my job was to dispense my hard-won wisdom about life via three-minute webcam videos. The other girls who worked for the site were hot but dumb. One fellow vlogger would routinely lose her train of thought and would randomly start dancing in the middle of her videos. Two minutes of lucid thought was too hard for her, apparently. With that kind of competition, I quickly became the most popular contributor. Those who can't do, teach!

Trojan once again entered my life when my boss at Double Agent, Charles, brokered an advertising deal with the company, which included an agreement to have a Double Agent girl host Trojan-sponsored parties around the country. Being that I was one of the few who could form coherent sentences, I had a brief phone call with a Trojan rep, who was baffled and delighted by my extensive knowledge of the brand (I even knew where their corporate headquarters were—Princeton, New Jersey) and insisted that I be the one to host the parties. Charles readily agreed, mostly because I was the only vlogger who seemed like she could use a condom without somehow getting trapped in it.

A few weeks later I was on a plane to New Orleans to host a fete during Jazz Fest. Trojan had rented out a huge nightclub for the event to lure in hoards of young, sexually active college kids. They even set up huge, carnival-like displays in the street. There was a wheel you could spin to win lube and vibrating rings, a tour bus filled with condom quiz games, even a bounce house! My job was to wear a tight, short dress and fanny around, interviewing hot girls about safe sex and why condoms are awesome.

Of my performance at said duties, I will say this: I may be a horrible reporter, but I'm a great interviewer. I can coax odd, hilarious, wildly inappropriate comments out of almost anyone. Hell, I could get the Pope to sing the *Fresh Prince of Bel Air* theme song if I really tried. So asking a bunch of drunk sluts to talk about banging dudes was cake. Delicious cake. Red velvet cake still warm from the oven and covered with frosting, but ooooh, the frosting is melting and dripping down the sides onto my hand, I'd better get—I'm sorry, what was I talking about? Oh, right. Interviews. The Trojan people were thrilled that I was getting such good sound bites, and soon I was booked to host another party in Boston, and several more in other cities. They paid me a few thousand dollars for each one, too—more than Kim Kardashian was making at the time, thankyouverymuch— but the *real* prize was the condom goodie bag they sent me after each event. I had forgotten all about the cache of rubbers lying under my bed until, several weeks after that first New Orleans party, a big box arrived at my apartment. Inside was a Trojan-branded backpack filled to the brim with prophylactic delights. Lube! Vibrating rings! Magnums! XLs! Ultra Thins! Oh my!

I've always been a bit greedy (the curse of being an only child), and suddenly I was feverish with glee at the thought of how many condoms I had amassed. My Scrooge McDuck fantasy sprang back to life, the painful memory of the post-breakup condom delivery was banished to the back of my brain, and my collection started to become a point of weird hoarder pride. Like a kid saving her pennies for a new toy, I eagerly counted each new rubber and added it to my growing heap. But soon it wasn't just Trojans I hoarded; I began collecting condoms of all varieties at every possible chance. I'd take fistfuls of free Durexes from the clinic and swipe errant Lifestyles from my guy friends' dressers. By the time my duties as Trojan spokesperson finished and I finally managed to pull the plug on my compulsive condom-snatching, I had amassed over 2,300 condoms. A quick calculation told me that a person would need to have sex more than six times a day for a year to use them up. And that's not even factoring in the gallons of lube and army of vibrating rings also stowed away, as though for some sort of sexual apocalypse.

By now I had taken up hockey, and all my available storage space was being occupied by extra gloves and pucks and Under Armour; I had no more room for all my rubbers. I briefly made the mistake of trying to store the two together . . . until a Magnum XL dropped out of my glove and onto the ice during a game. I lived in a spacious four-bedroom apartment in Chelsea with my friends Holly, Pfeiffer, and Marcia. But my roommates didn't much appreciate my stuffing Ultra Thins in every nook and cranny around the house. I had to get rid of them. Begrudgingly, I tried giving them out as stocking stuffers and birthday presents and including them in gift baskets, but even still, I was barely making a dent in my supply. I had so many, I didn't even bother storing them in duffel bags anymore; I just tossed them under the bed and vacuumed around them. Once they started to spill out from beneath my bed like dust bunnies the girls put their feet down.

"You're just going to have to start using them," Marcia said with a shrug, but it sounded impossible. Between work, sleep, showering, and eating, there was no way I could fit in six sexual romps a day. I didn't even have a boyfriend! And then, I had an idea . . . .

"No," I said, "*we* are going to start using them."

She stared at me for a long moment. "Look, I don't know what you have in mind, Shallon, but count me out."

I was talking about water balloon fights. It was summer and no one we knew had a pool, so what better way to make our own splish-splashy fun? Holly and Marcia and I went up to the roof one sticky afternoon with a box of Ultra Thins, prepared to cool off *and* pare down my mountain of cock socks.

Unfortunately, condoms make lousy water balloons. No, let me rephrase—they make *enormous* lousy water balloons. If you fill them to a manageable size, they're practically indestructible. But if you make them big enough to pop, they're too big to throw. They're too big to hold, actually; condoms filled with water look like huge amniotic sacs, wobbling and gurgling like an alien pod. Plus, they're all slippery with lube, so even if we managed to corral one in our arms, it would just wiggle right out, lumbering down the sloping roof and onto the pavement four stories below.

Splort!

We cringed, crouching down behind the air-conditioning unit, and prayed no one was hurt by our Trojan waterbomb. Clearly this wasn't working out as planned. We packed up our remaining rubbers, slunk back down to our apartment, and avoided looking out the window lest we discover a very dead, very wet body on the sidewalk.

With water balloon fights out of the question, I had only two remaining viable options for getting rid of all my jimmy hats: fill them with heroin and become a drug mule, or get a boyfriend. I have a small esophagus, so I chose the latter.

A few weeks later I started going out with Richie, a banker. At least I think he was. I didn't really pay much attention, but I know he worked in finance. He could've been the guy refilling the deposit slips at an ATM; I didn't really care. He was sexually active and that was all I needed to know. My roommates set us up, which at the time seemed like an altruistic gesture, but now I realize that it was more like a colossal practical joke. Richie and I were a horrible match; he slicked his hair back like Gordon Gekko and used phrases like "The talent in here is ridiculous" to indicate that a bar had a lot of pretty girls. But he had a good body. I didn't really need to like his personality, I reasoned, as long as he put out.

Now, you would think that finding a guy willing to sleep with a non-hunchbacked, dentally hygienic girl would not be difficult. But Richie was very odd. Very odd indeed.

While most bankers are full of swagger and bravado, Richie was skittish and paranoid. He'd cancel dates at the last minute. He'd incessantly look over his shoulder. And it was nearly impossible to get a straight answer out of him about anything, whether you asked him about his family or what time it was.

I wouldn't have cared so much if this jumpiness didn't translate to the bedroom as well. Making out was almost impossible—the second it got hot and heavy he would leap up to check his Black-Berry or rifle aimlessly through a drawer.

I thought about my stash of condoms, ticking away like a time bomb under the bed, begging to be used.

"What are you *doing*?" I'd say, sighing exasperatedly. "We are *never* going to get to third base if you keep rambling around!"

Even the way he kissed me was indecisive, his tongue darting around like a scared fish. Finally I just gave up on frenching alto-gether and settled for awkward, open-mouth, tongue-less kisses. It was like making out with a lead pipe.

Despite this madness, I still thought that perhaps he could be my Trojan prince. Maybe he just needed to get naked and then all the pieces would fall into place. But slowly I began to realize that Richie was . . . *a prude.*

No matter how many times I tried to seal the deal, he some-how wriggled out of my embrace, just like my ill-advised condom water balloons. WTF was his problem? He wasn't religious, or hold-ing out because he wanted us to get to know each other (I can't even remember his last name), or because he respected me sooooo much. I'm a patient woman, but it had been three weeks and I hadn't even seen him shirtless! That might've been okay if he had a glitter-ing personality with which to distract me. But no conversation *and* no nakedness? Nuh-uh. Not gonna fly with me. I had Magnums to use up.

Finally, fed up with his priggish baloney, I decided to get him good and drunk and drag him home like a caveman. I was a girl on a mission, an intrepid general flanked by her legion of rubbers, ready for action!

I plied him with tequila shots and lured him back to my house so I could begin my seduction, and at first, he seemed to comply. I peeled off his shirt, then his pants, my head swimming with victory. Things were looking good, *very* good, until Richie paused, saying he needed to turn off his phone.

"I just don't want us to be interrupted." He smiled and leaned over the side of the bed, grabbing for his BlackBerry, which had fallen on the floor.

I lay there on the bed, smiling serenely and looking at his perfect form in the moonlight, until . . .

"Umm, why do you have all these condoms?"

Oh. No. He must've been able to see under the bed and had discovered my treasure trove of contraceptives.

"I—I'm a spokesperson for Troj—" I stammered, but it was too late. Before I could even reach for him Richie had thrown his shirt on, backward; yanked on his pants, sans boxer briefs; and was halfway out the door. Wide-eyed and disgusted, he ran out so fast he practically left a Richie-shaped hole in the wall.

The next day, one of our mutual friends told me that Richie had shown up that night at his house, frantic and wasted, his underpants clutched tightly in his hand, babbling about rubbers. It's one thing to get rejected; it's another to have a man literally flee like he's being chased by bees.

"I think maybe it's time you give this condom thing up," Holly told me. "Can't you just donate them or something?"

I scowled. As charitable as I usually was, I had an odd attachment to my pile of prophyls. I had worked hard for them, after all. I hated the thought of turning my stash over to my local AIDS charity, even though clearly they could use them far more than the rumpled fedora from last season that I had ready to donate.

But I trotted a few hundred of the things down there anyway, ignoring the puzzled yet grateful stares of the volunteers. As I walked home, I felt somewhat lighter and happier knowing that I'd helped others . . . and yet I was still nettled at the way the Richie affair had gone. It wasn't just the way he left that was nagging me; why had he been so nervous and twitchy the entire time?

The answer came a few weeks later, in the form of an e-mail forward from our guy friend Beef.

"LOLZ!" he wrote. "Thought I recognized that face! Dude don't let your boss see this!"

It was a grainy X-rated porn screen cap featuring a busty, familiar-looking blonde writhing around with some toy that looked like a baseball bat.

WTF? I thought, scrolling down to the beginning of the thread.

Lo and behold, Richie had started the thread nearly a week before, sending it out to over forty people, many of whom I knew.

"Yo playaz," he wrote in the original message, "this is the condom chick I was telling you about. I KNEW she looked familiar, right?! Thanks for finding this pic bro. What a slut, totally dodged a bullet there."

Wait a minute. Wait. Does he think that I . . . ? Does that girl look like . . . ? *Oh my god.*

Suddenly it all made sense—his prudishness, his reluctance to tell me any personal information, the total freak-out over the rubbers. He thought I was a porn star! Honestly, how *anyone* could mistake me and my B-cups for an adult performer was beyond me. But Richie wasn't the brightest bulb and had assumed that my "writing" career was a euphemism for something else. For him, the stockpile of condoms under the bed was the last piece of the puzzle.

After that, my friends expected me to wash my hands of my stash once and for all, but those jimmy hats were all that I had left. My boy, my reputation, my pride—they were all gone. Like a fading actress clinging to her old costumes and fineries, I kept the rubbers as a reminder of a better time, when boys actually *wanted* to sleep with me. To this day, I have enough condoms to keep me occupied well into middle age. But sometimes, when I start dating someone I really, really like, I'll trot down to the store and buy a shiny new package, just for him. I want him to know that he's special enough to deserve it, that I'm not just sleeping with him to whittle down my stockpile . . . but God help that douchebag if he dumps me before we use up the pack. I'll pull a Magnum XL over his head 'til he suffocates.

Still, I have yet to figure out which is worse—getting mistaken for a professional tramp or realizing that even then, I still couldn't get laid.

My Chemical (Peel) Romance

Having a fervent, obsessive, teenybopper crush on a celebrity is cute when you're thirteen. But when you're twenty-five, it's just creepy.

I was never one of those little girls who thought boys were icky or had cooties. Instead, they were like a car crash on the other side of the freeway—dangerous and thrilling. I wanted to get closer and see what exactly these odd, grubby creatures were all about. But even at the tender age of five, I realized pretty quickly that it would be a number of years before the boys my age would catch up with me; there was no way little Joe Claytor or Eddie Lee could handle Shallon Lester, vixen in OshKosh B'gosh.

So I turned my attention to men who would surely be worthy: celebrities.

By first grade, I was convinced that Tom Cruise was my future husband. At the time, I had only a vague idea of what sex was—I was pretty sure it involved some sort of elaborate dance and a special pair of shoes—but I knew that one day, I'd do it with the *Top Gun* star.

When I was eight, my focus shifted to Garth Brooks. He was well on his way to balding and a middle-aged paunch, but I thought he was just dreamy. I blanketed my room with his posters and tortured my mom with his music.

But even then monogamy wasn't my strong suit and I wasn't faithful to Garth. I had a side thing going with the douchey lead singer of Color Me Badd until I beheld the majesty, the luminous glory, of Axl Rose.

The full scope of my Guns N' Roses fixation is too embarrassing to detail, but let's just say no one in my family will ever look at a bandana or pair of leggings the same way again.

Mama assumed that the death of hair metal would also spell the end of my ridiculous celebrity mania, but no such luck. I was like a serial killer whose crimes slowly escalated.

After Axl came a years-long devotion to Green Day, followed by unsettling obsessions with Vince Vaughn, Prince William, and Gavin Rossdale. Freshman year of college I slept with a framed picture of Josh Hartnett next to my bed, and by junior year my room had become a shrine to Joaquin Phoenix.

There's no way to pinpoint which of my celebrity obsessions were the most fervent, because they *all* were. *Everyone* was a Beatle.

But then I met Ryan, and for three years the Hartnetts and Phoenixes took a backseat to a real-life slice of adulation. I hoped that finding actual, tangible love would end my teenybopper fever, and for a while it did. I no longer skulked incognito around Barnes & Noble to buy every *Tiger Beat* or *Bop* magazine and had removed (almost) every Jude Law RSS feed from my laptop.

But like Axl Rose's ill-advised hair extensions, things fell apart. We broke up and I moved to New York, a city that has a way of undoing your sanity, bit by bit.

I can't say for sure why I fell in love with Alex. He was nineteen, had a huge nose, and lived in the NYU dorms. Not exactly the knight in shining Varvatos I'd envisioned as my debonair New York suitor, but after two dates I was ready to marry him. Alex had swooped into my life at exactly the right time, like Dumbledore's phoenix, saving me just when I needed it the most.

I had been in Manhattan for a year and finally climbed out of the minimum-wage tar pit that was my waitressing job at Houston's. I was six weeks into my job at *FHM* as assistant editor and had just scored a book deal for my first book, *Hot Mess*. By all accounts, my dreams were coming true.

And yet, something felt . . . missing. Something was beginning to stir within me, like there was another Shallon waiting to get out. Maybe it was the bittersweet restlessness that came with reaching a goal and realizing it wasn't enough to keep you happy forever. Or maybe my newfound success was unearthing dimensions of my personality that had never felt confident enough to come out.

Once upon a time, I discussed politics and books and art, things not involving fake boobs whatsoever. But the deeper I got into *FHM*'s world of beer and porn, and the more time I spent crafting bubblegum fiction, the more hungry I became for *real* conversation.

It was like I had intellectual scurvy and was slowly rotting without proper nutrition.

That's when I met him. Yes, he was young (very, *very* young), but he struck me as an old soul. His mother wrote magical realism novels and had dinner with Joni Mitchell. Alex and I talked about our dreams and our goals and where we hoped New York, and life, would take us. It had been months since I'd had such deep conversations with someone, and my malnourished mind gobbled it up.

But some things that feed you can also be bad for you, like a tuna sandwich that's been sitting out too long. After a few dates I could feel him pulling away, catching whiffs of my scary, restraining-order-type love. I knew I should tone it down, but I just couldn't. God wanted me to love him, I told myself. Well, I was half-right. God wanted me to love him, but more importantly, God also wanted him to *not* love me back.

I had definitely loved other boys deeper and longer, but for some reason, Alex's departure hit me like a ton of bricks.

"Muuu-hu-hu-hu!" I sobbed to my friends at brunch. "Alex is gone! Gonnnnne! Wuuu-hu-hu-hu!"

They patted my hand and went back to their mini muffins, assuming that this was just another melodramatic faux breakup with a faux boyfriend. But after three months of mourning, no one knew what to do with me.

"I'm no mathematician," said Klo, "but you realize that you've been crying over him four times longer than you actually knew him, right?"

Marcia pointed out that I hadn't even been this upset when John cheated on me six months prior.

But there was a difference. I had always known John was a square peg in a round hole (more like a three-inch peg, but that's another story); I knew in my heart we were never meant to work, I just kept trying anyway. But Alex had felt right from the very start. Since my friends clearly weren't going to indulge me, I sequestered myself in my apartment for yet *another* night and sulked.

I flipped on the TV and landed on Fuse, an alt-music channel playing a block of videos from a screechy band called My Chemical Romance. And just like that, my world began to look bright again. It was as if an angel floated into my living room. A pale, stringy-haired, pudgy-around-the-middle angel named Gerard Way, the band's lead singer. He was a cross between Jack White and Dracula and utterly perfect in every way. After thirty seconds I knew that this celebrity fascination would trump all others; it would Bieber where the rest had merely Jonathan Taylor Thomased.

The band's funeral-themed video for "Helena" was morose, bizarre, and self-indulgent . . . and the most magical thing I'd ever seen. Gerard's intensity, his hopelessness—it all just spoke to me. In rapt awe, I watched all six videos on TV, then again (and again and again) on YouTube.

My roommate Holly came home and I asked her if she'd heard of My Chemical Romance.

"Yeah, I think so," she said, taking off her J.Crew cardigan. "They're that emo band with that vampire singer, right?"

"But they're so much *more* than that!" I blurted before I could stop myself. Seeing Gerard had been a religious awakening, a beacon to some promised land.

This creepy little band from the New Jersey badlands had tapped into a part of myself that I hadn't even realized existed: the dark, dreamy, gothic Shallon that lurked beneath my peppy surface. In retrospect, perhaps the appeal of it was that it seemed forbidden; I was supposed to be fun! And bubbly! And blond! I wore pastel, not crushed purple velvet. In high school, the only kids who ever got teased were the Goths, a pathetic collection of fat, pasty freaks in black dresses who drifted around the campus looking like deranged nuns. No one could ever understand WTF they were so ticked off about anyway. Being unattractive? Big deal! The world is full of other ugly people for them to date and hang out with—statistically, they're on the winning end.

Maybe a Goth makeover was just what I needed! At first my preppy self recoiled at the idea of this whole Goth/emo thing, but after weeks of weeping over Alex, I had wrung all the consolation I could from my depressing Beyoncé playlists. I had to try *something*. In my youth, I didn't have the means to transform my personality with every new celebrity crush; it's hard to afford that Garth Brooks Stetson, rawhide boots, and belt buckle on a $10-a-week allowance. But now, as a freewheelin' adult, I could pour every cent, minute, and breath into my *new* true purpose in life: My Chemical Romance.

I threw myself into the band with a zeal I hadn't felt since my Guns N' Roses days. I learned lyrics and stats, joined discussion groups, and drained my office's color printer to cover my bedroom with pictures of Gerard and his smoking-hot guitarist Frank Iero.

Then there was the issue of my wardrobe. My closet full of frilly tops and sundresses suddenly repulsed me, as did the sunny disposition of my roommates. I wanted to be around my depressed equals but was never going to find "my people" if I didn't make a break (at least temporarily) from my crew of ex-sorority girls.

"Ladies," I announced to my friends during our weekly get-together to watch *The Bachelor*, "I have an announcement. I am no longer preppy . . . I am emo. I am going to start wearing a lot of black, and hoodies and skinny jeans. So there."

"So you never want to have sex again is what you're saying?" quipped Pfeiffer.

Holly chimed in. "Yeah, I'm not sure that making yourself as ugly as possible is going to help you find another dude."

"I don't care," I said indignantly. "Maybe I *do* need a break from guys. All I know is that I'm unhappy and this makes me feel better. I want to be as ugly on the outside as I feel on the inside."

"Well whatever," Marcia said. "Just don't start shopping at Hot Topic."

The truth was, I'd tried to shop at Hot Topic but didn't have the guts to actually go in. I could sashay into Chanel just fine, but in Hot Topic, I felt the rare, humiliating sensation of being an outsider. And I didn't like it one bit.

Finally, after pacing back and forth past the Harry Potter jewelry, studded corsets, and hot-pink fishnets in the front window for twenty minutes, I mustered up the courage to enter—well armed with a lie, of course.

"Hi," I said nervously to the pierced guy behind the counter. "I'm looking for some stuff for my little sister . . . who is exactly the same size as me. But she isn't me. Really."

I shopped skittishly, constantly eyeing the door expecting someone I knew to walk in and nab me like on an episode of *To Catch a Predator*. After fifteen jumpy minutes, I left with two My Chem shirts, a Fall Out Boy hoodie, and several bits of *Twilight* paraphernalia. And . . . a fake lip ring. I'd wanted to pierce my lip for years, but Pfeiffer said she'd call my grandma Gigi if I did, so this was our compromise.

That night, I debuted my new emo look, lip ring and all.

"Oh, Shallon, it's *so* ugly!" Pfeiffer gasped, but I didn't care. I felt more like myself than I had in months. Every ounce of sullenness that had been buried beneath pep rallies and sorority parties was at last allowed to blossom in all of its black glory.

I rewatched all of Angelina Jolie's interviews from her Gothy period, feeling just like her—deep and misunderstood, having no choice but to conceal any sort of natural beauty under too-pale makeup and dark lipstick. I felt a special kinship with her lower-belly tattoo reading "*Quod me nutrit me destruit*"—*That which nourishes me also destroys me.*

But a girl cannot survive on Angelina alone. Miraculously, my friends were still letting me hang out with them, hoodie and all, but I needed a partner in crime—an emo boyfriend.

Obviously my first choice was Gerard, but I didn't really have the time or energy to find his house in Jersey and sit outside it until I could kidnap him. A substitute would have to do.

"Attention, gentlemen!" I hollered to the dudes in my office, and held up a copy of *AP* magazine with Gerard on the cover. "I demand to be set up with someone who looks like *this*!"

After explaining that Gerard was neither a girl nor a character from Harry Potter, I demanded that they cull their circle of friends to find me a doppelganger.

"Why don't you just date the intern?" said Tom, our web designer. "He kinda looks like him I guess. And he's young, just how you like 'em—he turns nineteen next week."

"Gimme."

It was our summer intern Keith's first day, and as an initiation, someone had sent him on a run to buy the latest issues of *Penthouse* and *Hustler*. I hadn't met him yet and waited like a sexual predator in the lobby for him to return. He walked through the door, the porno mags peeking out of his messenger bag, and took my breath away. He looked *exactly* like Gerard—dark shaggy hair, blazing green eyes, and a mischievous smile. Keith was thirty pounds lighter and had a bit of a tan, but I was willing to overlook it. This teenage dreamboat was clearly a gift from a kind, benevolent God, and I was not about to get greedy.

Nor was I about to play it cool. Even now, years later, Keith loves to remind me of how I first hit on him in the elevator.

"You know," I said, trying to sound offhanded, "you look an awful lot like that guy from My Chemical Romance. Has anyone ever told you that?"

He just laughed nervously and shrugged, saying that he didn't know who that was. Within five minutes of being back at my desk I had sent Keith a few of Gerard's (relatively) less weird pictures and videos and we struck up an e-mail exchange. Beneath his adolescent nervousness, Keith actually had a tremendous amount of game. He was smart and cavalier and hadn't yet learned how terrifying girls can be, so he had no fear when it came to pursuing me. For the next couple of weeks we flirted constantly and e-mailed all day long. But as the only girl in the office, I was not about to flush my hard-won reputation down the toilet by shagging some teenager in the fashion closet, so for once, I bided my time.

On the interns' last day we took them out for celebratory Irish Car Bombs, and that was when Keith, fueled by Baileys and Guinness, finally made his move. I was regaling the boys with tales of my many sexual calamities when he staggered up, grabbed me by the back of the neck, and said, "You've just never been with a real man!" and planted a kiss on me.

The guys high-fived him as I feigned offense and embarrassment, but really, I was delighted—I loved aggressive boys. I'd targeted Keith to sublimate my desire for Gerard, but maybe I'd found something even better! That weekend, I let Keith take me on a date. We ate spaghetti and then went for a drive; I hadn't been in a non-taxi car in months, and I was in heaven the minute I scooted into his SUV.

"Where do you want to go?" he said softly, slipping his hand into mine slowly and meaningfully, the way *I* used to before I devoured boys like kebobs.

"I don't care," I purred. "Let's go get lost."

We zigzagged across the city in the cool summer twilight and meandered out to his hometown in Jersey to look at the massive houses. It was a simple date—dinner and a drive, holding hands and listening to the radio—but the simple life can be hard to come by in Manhattan.

When I told him about my emo revolution, he gently mocked me.

"Who are you kidding?" he laughed. "You're the girliest girl I've ever met! You can wear ten hoodies but it's always going to look phony on you. You're meant for pink and dresses."

"I am not!" I said like an indignant four-year-old. "I *am so* gloomy and Gothy!"

"All right, princess." He smiled, stroking my cheek. "Whatever makes you happy."

As unlikely as it was, Keith and I just seemed to fit. He, like Alex, was boyish and exuberant yet wise beyond his years. We spent as much time together as we could, but two weeks later, he was packing up his Toyota and heading back to school.

"Will you come visit?" he asked, and I made feeble promises I knew I'd never keep. With my new look I felt out of place enough hanging out with my own friends in my own city; I wasn't about to take my freak show on the road.

I gave him a kiss good-bye, but as I watched him inch away through the midtown traffic, a wrenching feeling settled over me.

Quod me nutrit, me destruit.

Hoping it would numb the pain over losing Keith the way it had with Alex, I lay on the couch that night in the dark and watched the video for MCR's "Helena," where a church full of mourners dance eerily around a dead woman as the band plays dramatically from the pulpit. What fun! No matter how depressed I was, watching "Helena" would usually cheer me up, if for no other reason than the sick pleasure I get from planning my own funeral (everyone is going to wear white and eat enchiladas). Plus, it reminds me that whatever pain I'm feeling can't possibly last forever—one day I'll meet the sweet release of death and then no one can reject or criticize or pester me to please use a coaster because I'm getting water spots on the coffee table.

But that night, Gerard's yelping melodrama didn't lift my spirits at all. During the end scene, where they carry the casket out and into the hearse, I had a thunderously gloomy thought: *If I died tomorrow, who would be my pallbearers?* The only man I could come up with was Keith, *if* he wasn't tied up with midterms or an Ultimate Frisbee tourney. The next morning, after wracking my brain for twelve hours, I managed to add my gay friend Sam and his boyfriend to the list. That's only half as many as you need.

Great, I thought, wallowing around in my sheets, *I'll die and my bulky casket will have to be* dragged *out of the church. It'll be like the way you just heave a suitcase down stairs when you're too lazy to carry it and don't really know or care if anything breakable is inside. Then you get really nettled when you open it up and find that your Gucci glasses were smashed to bits and blame TSA instead of yourself.*

That was no way to leave this world. I would need the full number of pallbearers. I briefly considered the guys in my office, but they were web geeks and not very burly. And our friendships weren't really at the "Hey, will you carry my lifeless body to the graveyard?" stage yet.

I picked up the phone to call Keith but decided against it. I needed to let him escape while he still could. I called Klo instead.

"I'm confused," she said. "Do you want to *date* Gerard Way or *be* him?"

I paused, not really sure myself. Yes, I found him insanely, irresistibly, inexplicably sexy, but I also envied his solipsistic vanity.

He screamed and wailed about his problems like they were what sank the *Titanic*.

I wondered if I'd been going about this whole celebrity crush thing all wrong for the last twenty years. Did I really love *any* of them? Or did I simply envy them because they were famous and drunk on the freedom to be weird, slutty, outspoken, and self-indulgent?

It was about time I found out.

I tried to look at Gerard as objectively as possible and pinpoint our differences. If I could close the gap maybe I could break free from my celeb fanaticism once and for all. Turns out, Gerard and I were very much alike: we had both been dorky teenagers, were oddly close with our grandmothers, and cared a little too much about the X-Men. But the one disparity I couldn't get around? Our skin tone.

After college, I briefly worked at a tanning salon and quickly got the message that staying out of the sun is your only shot at looking young forever. The patrons of BareTan looked more like saddles than people, so from then on I slathered my French-Italian skin in SPF 70 at all times. Being blond, I looked good pale, like an Aryan propaganda poster. But even at my New York winter whitest, I was nowhere near Gerard's ghostly pallor. He looked like the underside of a deep-sea fish. I had a lot of work to do.

"If you want to get pale," said my trainer Reggie, "you talk to the Puerto Ricans. Those girls *hate* their skin and they've got all sorts of creams to whiten themselves up."

I took a train out to Spanish Harlem that night and chatted up the around-the-way girls at the local beauty shop.

"*Mami*, whatchu need is this right heeah," said one, handing me a jar of Nadinola Fade Cream. "Dis'll get ju white in no time, juknowwhatI'msayin'?"

The stuff smelled like Styrofoam peanuts, but I lathered myself up twice a day, just like Esmerelda and Vivi had suggested. Within a week I had seen a small improvement in my paleness, at least judging by the comments I was getting at work.

"Jesus, you look awful," said our new intern, Steve, while the HR lady left packets of Emergen-C on my desk every afternoon.

Looking sickly and tubercular was a small bit of success, but I wanted to be positively vampirish. I wanted to look like something Stephenie Meyer dreamed up—minus all that gay sparkling, of course. I knew it was time for something drastic yet strangely fitting: a chemical peel.

My dermatologist back home had suggested it once before, and it sounded ugly and painful—three days of blistering, peeling skin—but since ugly and painful was my new autumn look, I was all for it.

Luckily, I had a trip to Irvine coming up, so I booked an appointment. "Kinda ironic, isn't it?" my doctor said with a wry smile as he painted my face with the caustic goo. "You come to Southern California to get pale. Seems like Wisconsin would've been the logical choice!"

"Just gimme the juice, doc!" I said through gritted teeth like a heroin addict or a death row inmate strapped to the chair. *And in a way*, I told myself morosely, *this procedure is like a death. After, I shall be reborn as a true emo kid, pale, like a ghost drifting around New York, haunting it with my lameness.*

What I was reborn as was in fact a cross between a molting pigeon and a boiled hot dog. My skin peeled off in penny-sized pieces, littering the front of my shirt with flakes. But of course it didn't all shed at the same time or in any sort of pattern. So while one part of my face looked like it was snowing, another quadrant was still bright red and too tight to move. I looked like Jonah Hex, and Mama was horrified.

"Shallon, please, *please* stay in the car," she begged, pulling up to the supermarket.

"Nur!" I gurgled through the corner of my mouth, which was still too tight to open. "I'ng going wiffoo."

She relented, pulling the hood on my grim reaper sweatshirt up and drawing the strings so tight it looked like I was being born. For good measure, she fished an ancient "Hanu Reddy Realty" cap out of the glove compartment and added it to the mix. All you could see were my nose and mouth, but that was more than enough to terrify.

"Just get enough waffle mix and syrup for the next few days so you won't have to leave the house," she told me, and once inside the market she took off like a greyhound. I couldn't blame her for not wanting to be seen with me, a blond Frankenstein lurching around the produce section.

"Affulshs?" I asked a teenage stockboy. "I eed affulshs. Un sirp."

He recoiled in horror and thrust an Entenmann's Danish at me the way one might toss a rotisserie chicken to a zombie hell-bent on eating one's brain.

"Affulshs, sirp," I grunted, and lumbered back to the safety of our Honda, chuckling at the irony.

Here I was, burning off my own skin to quell my emo itch, to feed my bizarre hunger to wear my depression on the outside. No one seemed to understand why, and if I had to put my finger on it, I couldn't either. This emo revolution was a biological need so strong I couldn't ignore it. I was sure that there was some greater purpose; I just didn't know what yet.

Four days later, I emerged from blistering hideousness as a porcelain-skinned butterfly. Delighted, I put dark red streaks in my hair to look even paler, splurged on some black Chanel nail polish, and stocked up on leather leggings. I flew home to New York like

Caesar riding back across the Rubicon into Rome. I was going to conquer this new social scene come hell or high-waisted pants.

And triumph I did. With my shored-up wardrobe and cadaverous complexion, I had the confidence to drag Klo to Black and White, an East Village bar overflowing with indie rockers and emos.

And it was there that I would meet . . . *him*. There, like Gaius Julius Caesar, I would draw someone close to me who would eventually be my undoing: Lord Voldemort.

Quod me nutrit, me destruit.

Dignity on Sale, Aisle Five!

What's worse than running into your ex while serving Awesome Blossoms to tourists? Worse than running into not just any ex, but *the* ex of all exes—the grand high wizard of heartbreak and evil, Lord Voldemort?

Running into him when you're bargain shopping. In sweatpants!

It was a sweltering August afternoon and I was creeping around Loehmann's, as I tended to do that summer. A few weeks prior we had finished filming *Downtown Girls,* and I had nothing to do during the days—no office job, no kids to mind, no felony conviction to serve community service for.

Fortunately, neither did my best friend, Klo, who was just as bored and cheap as I was. So we spent the humid days lurking around town, making our daily rounds to T.J. Maxx, Loehmann's, and, if we were feeling adventurous, the Target in Brooklyn. If we scored a particularly awesome deal, we'd celebrate by drinking a bottle of whiskey at Angels and Kings, the bar her fiancé owned.

The only real structure I had to my day was seeing my trainer. Reggie Chambers was a hulking black man who looked like he would love nothing more than to see you do bicep curls until you vomited, but instead he was quick to smile and had a lot of tolerance for my complaining and lack of natural athleticism. He was tasked with whipping me into camera-ready shape, and sometimes I didn't know who I felt sorrier for—him for taking on such a difficult assignment, or me for having to endure it.

Every morning I'd emerge from High Performance Fitness ratty and covered in sweat. My producers would beg me not to trot around town looking so terrifying, but *pffft*, who was I going to see? Anyone who mattered was at work, right?

Klo happened to be busy that day, so I rode my bike, Amelia, down to Loehmann's alone and prowled around for . . . something. Nothing. I didn't need anything, mostly because I didn't *do* anything. Everyone thought my life post-filming was soooo glamorous, but mostly I skulked around the city, watched endless episodes of *Degrassi: The Next Generation*, and waited to hear news of when *Downtown Girls* would air. I didn't need clothes for work or dates because I was involved in neither. What was I even doing at Loehmann's?

Just as I was about to head home, a sparkly pair of Steve Madden heels caught my eye; someone had abandoned them right there in the plus-sized section I had wandered into, and as I stooped down to grab them—my size too!—I felt a ripple of good luck. The feeling would not last long.

As I crouched down, I looked up and saw the boy who had destroyed my heart two years prior, Lord Voldemort. So many thoughts filled my head at once, I felt like I was having a stroke. *Where did he come from?! What is he doing in the fatty section of Loehmann's?! Did he see me?!* Our eye contact lasted but a millisecond, but it was too late; a dam had burst in my mind, and the memories of our doomed love came flooding back.

Voldy and I had met one brisk spring evening at an indie rock bar that I'd begun frequenting on account of my emo revolution. Within a few weeks I was head over heels.

He was funny and clever and loved all the same dorky things that I did. For weeks we e-mailed back and forth, pages and pages at a time. In the first blush of our courtship, I presented him with the same all-important question I posed to every guy I dated: Which X-Man would you be?

I had long ago settled on Magneto, who could control metal, because metal is everywhere. I would stop car accidents and yank metal fillings out of my enemies' mouths!

I could tell a lot about a man based on what X-Man he chose. The ones who picked Wolverine were invariably macho man-children with a lot more ego than brains. But really good in bed.

Some said Gambit because he had a cool N'Awlins accent and was good at poker. That was acceptable, I suppose, but those boys seemed less like well-endowed superheros and more like shifty Tulane frat boys.

And then there was one dude who picked Storm—who is a woman.

"You'd be the *girl*?" I said, my voice dripping with revulsion. "The girl who makes it rain?"

He balked. "What? That'd be really useful!"

"Yeah if you were a goddamn park ranger." I snorted. "How does that make you a *hero*?"

Clearly it didn't, neither in the world of Marvel comics nor in my bedroom.

But Voldemort's answer trumped them all.

"Oh! I've totally thought of this before!" he wrote. "I'd be a new one called Element. He could control earth, wind, water, and fire."

"Isn't that Captain Planet?"

"Eh, I feel like he's more about recycling than doing cool stuff."

Voldy and I went back and forth debating the virtues of Element versus Magneto. I argued that Element would be little more than a fancied-up Storm, but when he countered that the ubiquity of plastic would soon make me useless, my heart melted.

We even made up stories about what life would be like in the Element/Magneto household—*our* household, the superhero one that we had started to build in our minds.

We even had a fictitious dog, Waffles, and spent pages detailing how we would dupe each other into picking up his poop. Element's plan was to feed him an iron-rich diet so the scat, now mostly metal, would fall into my domain.

I saved each and every one of those e-mails. I printed them out to give to him, all pretty and bound into a book, on some quiet wedding anniversary.

My friends just rolled their eyes and figured that Voldy wasn't much different than any other guy I'd dated. But they were wrong.

My love for Voldemort was quiet yet magnificent. It wasn't the manic, sugar-rushy adoration I had felt for other boys; it was like a great comforting yawn. It was happy and peaceful and true and shone like justice in the morning light.

Usually at the beginning of a relationship, I kept my fingers crossed and did rain dances hoping that things would work out. Not with Voldy. It seemed unnecessary. When I was with him, I felt a resolute nod from the universe that yep, this is the man you've been waiting for. He was why God had planned my emo revolution, the reason I'd endured caustic chemical peels and had all my pants tapered. All those things were the broken road that led to him, my northern star.

Or . . . not.

The pain I felt when I lost him was just as awesome, but in no way as silent.

A few months into the relationship, while on a trip to Miami, he had met and slept with a go-go dancer named Crystal. She was twenty-one, with a six-year-old kid and a drug conviction. The cruel irony was that everything that protruded on her body was made of plastic—nails, boobs, ass, lips. And he fell in love with her.

The day he called and told me, I literally collapsed. My legs just said, "Fuck this noise," and gave out, like I had polio. My roommate Holly found me like that an hour later, shaking and sobbing and writhing. She tried talking me down but I remember barely being able to hear her. The pain was deafening. It was needles between my eyes, liquefying every muscle in my body. He was *part of me*, not just some dude I was dating. No heartbreak in my entire life would compare to this. I was sure of it.

I stayed in more or less that crumpled state for *seven months*. Twenty-eight weeks of daily sobbing, 210 ten days of misery so acute it made me nauseous. I'm pretty sure this is how boys feel when someone kicks them in the balls.

In the morning, I would wake up with salty cheeks from the evaporated tears I'd shed in my sleep without knowing it. My body was so accustomed to the sound of my weeping that it barely even registered.

"It's just a fling," worried friends said of the crack whore, "he'll be back—they *always* come back."

But he didn't. Instead, he moved her to New York and they

bought a dog—*our* dog. Suddenly Element was playing house with Spandexia, a supervillain whose power was to shatter dreams with a single blow job.

And Magneto was out in the cold, trying in vain to pull her slutty, evil replacement out of his arms, but alas, the replacement was made of plastic. His prediction had been right—I had become useless.

Now all these years later here I was in the basement of Loehmann's, pretty much the same way he'd left me: on my knees and terrified.

This made the Giant Douche run-in look like an episode of *Touched by an Angel*.

I wasn't sure that he'd seen me but I had to get the hell out of that store—fast.

I dropped the shoes and slithered between the racks of clothes, backing toward the escalator. The other shoppers cocked their heads curiously at me. I looked like I was being chased by an alligator. I managed to weave through them and dart out of the store to Amelia, who was chained up across the street. I realized then and there that I should probably avoid a career in bank robbery and/or bomb defusing—maintaining steady hands under pressure is clearly not my forte.

After fumbling with the lock and cussing for several minutes, I hopped on and pedaled wildly into traffic. In my haste, one of my flip-flops fell off.

And I left it, like a wounded comrade too cumbersome to rescue. I cut my losses and glanced back at it lying pathetically in the road as I sped toward home.

A few minutes later, I was safe, back on my shady street, and I coasted to a stop in front of our local bar . . .

. . . where I bumped into Chace Crawford and Ed Westwick. Of course. *Of course.*

Chace's publicist was a friend of mine and had introduced me to him at a Super Bowl party. I had met loads of celebrities, but he literally took my breath away. He was flawless, charming, and gracious. At the party, the three of us had chit-chatted before he said he was calling it a night.

"That's a shame," I'd said, "you're going to miss out on some Irish Car Bombs!"

His eyes lit up. "Car Bombs?" he chirped. "Yes. Awesome. I'm in, let's go!"

We headed back inside and sidled up to some liquor. These twenty glorious and unexpected minutes of bar-side chatter immediately sparked countless fantasies in my mind that usually involved Chase shirtless, whipped cream, and a very large tarp.

Ed Westwick also ranked high on my Future Ex-Husbands dream list but seemed to be the polar opposite of boy-next-door Chace. Ed was swarthy and British and sexed up, the kind of guy for whom chest hair was a weapon of seduction. I had met him a few different times at various parties and had even trudged down to the East Village to see him sing with his dreadful band, the Filthy Youth.

These two heartthrobs were the reason my wardrobe was full of headbands and kicky plaid skirts, not to mention why I once blew an entire week's paycheck on lunch at the Plaza. Every girl in Manhattan, maybe the country, wanted to live like they did on *Gossip Girl*, the show that made it cool to be ruthless and wear tights! Who needs an X-Man when you can have an Archibald?

Any other day of the year, I would have given a kidney to run into these two. But right then, sweaty, half barefoot, and panicky over my encounter, I would've given a kidney to have a meteorite strike me dead.

But oh, Shallon, *no way* would these two dreamboats recognize you, right?

Fail.

"Oi, I know you . . . ," Ed drawled in his smoky English accent. "You're that bird from the newspaper . . ."

"N-nope, no I'm not," I stammered, still looking around in terror, worried Voldemort had followed me. "I'm not Sha—I'm not anyone. At all."

"Yeah, you know my publicist!" Chase said, chiming in. "I met you at the Super Bowl; we did Irish Car Bombs!"

I winced at the memory of a happier, cleaner, less grubby me.

"Wait," he said, suddenly looking down, "where's your shoe?"

At that exact moment, Cheryl, a homeless woman whom I had befriended, walked by and hollered my name. And pointed.

"Hey, Shallon! Shallon, over here! Hi!"

So there I was. Dirty, jumpy, shoeless, and apparently little miss popular among the homeless. Chace and Ed exchanged puzzled looks, trying to figure out what in the hell was going on.

I bit my lip miserably and instantly invented a thousand different low-rent superheroes I'd rather have been in that moment other than myself: Minestronia, able to shoot scalding hot soup or goulash from her fingertips! Or Tin Lizzie, whose can-opener claws will slice and dice her foes! Even Walruse, a mild-mannered Sea World employee by day, vengeful tusked pinniped by night!

But alas, I was just plain old Shallon, with the power to create humiliating situations with nothing more than a bike, an ex, and a dirty flip-flop.

Everyone but the Turtle

Usually, I make friends easily. I'm blond and feisty and can be quite charming when I want to be. But apparently, I'm a lot less enchanting dressed as an anthropomorphic amphibian.

Let me explain.

I never really got the memo that you were supposed to dress slutty for Halloween. Even as a child, when this wasn't yet expected, my costumes were weirder than everyone else's. This was quite an accomplishment considering the flock of geeks who went to Vista Verde ("Vista *Nerdy*"), my year-round K-8 school. On the cutting edge of liberal education, we were like a normal school on opposite day—the jocks were the least popular, the smart kids were never bullied, and Principal Terry always ran the jog-a-thon in a hula skirt. Vista Verde was the whole reason my mom moved us from San Francisco, the bohemian paradise she so loved, and her sacrifice paid off—the school was a total dork factory. The nine years I spent at VV were the best of my life, an idyllic, dweeby paradise that let my inherent oddness flourish like an orchid in a hothouse.

And flourish it did.

My last normal Halloween was in third grade. I went as a can-can girl—that is, I wore my dance recital costume and put on rouge. The next year, however, my mom spent weeks working on an elaborate court jester outfit that won our school's annual costume contest. I was thrilled . . . until someone put two and two together and came up with the nickname "Lester the Jester." I couldn't get too angry about it; the moniker made a lot of sense. Picture ten-year-old Shallon, just as sarcastic and awkward, but add in a fanatical love for *Zoobooks*, unicorn stickers, and *Reading Rainbow* and you got yourself one big doofus. And, just like any weirdo, Halloween was my time to shine. If there had been Comic-Con back then, I would've pwned that shit too.

Mama wasn't helping the situation, either. Most parents help steer their children *toward* sanity, but my mom (who didn't exactly fit the suburban mold herself) thought I was super-awesome in all my PBS quirkiness. She became my Halloween enabler.

In fifth grade, I was religiously into the Disney movie *The Sword in the Stone,* so Mama oh-so-helpfully suggested I go as Merlin for Halloween. The only thing more awkward would've been to dress as Archimedes the owl, but that costume was pretty intricate, so we settled for the next-creepiest thing. She fashioned a long, boxy gown out of dark blue fabric with gold stars, made a matching pointy hat, and whittled a wand from the Japanese maple in the backyard. But the coup de grâce was the fake beard. Mama was so concerned with authenticity, she probably would've consented to testosterone shots so I could grow the real thing. But instead, she spent thirty minutes carefully pasting fuzzy strands of gray batting, one by one, onto my face and eyebrows.

I'm not going to lie—I looked pretty great. There aren't many eleven-year-old girls who can pass for a geriatric wizard, you know. I netted a huge haul of candy and declared the night a glittering success . . . until I tried to get the beard *off*.

Soap, eye-makeup remover, Soft Scrub—nothing worked. Turns out, Mama had used some NASA-grade superglue. We even tried to shave it off, hoping that the razor could slide under the adhesive and scrape it off. Nothing. Already hopped up from mini Snickers bars, I had a panic attack. I pictured slinking into school the next day with facial hair and getting sent to the nurse's office on suspicion of a pituitary problem. Even at Vista Nerdy, that wasn't cool.

Finally, a mixture of turpentine and olive oil seemed to loosen the glue, and after two hours of scraping, I was free. My cheeks looked like I'd gotten into a slap fight with a rabid cat, but it was still better than a face full of hair. I vowed to stick to normal Halloween outfits—kitties, princesses, maybe the occasional ninja. Boring, sure, but I didn't care how many bite-sized Butterfingers it might cost me.

But time has a way of fading memories, and twelve months later I had managed to craft an equally bizarre Halloween costume: a head on a plate.

Yes, I'm afraid you read that right. I was in sixth grade and stoked for my very first school dance, which unfortunately happened to be a Halloween dance. While my friends planned to go as normal things like Nefertiti or a Gypsy, my mom latched on to the head-on-a-plate idea. It would be years before a drug-themed T-shirt taught me not to let my mom play stylist for school dances, so at this point I was still full of foolish trust.

The costume was simple: a piece of cardboard cut so that it could fit around my neck, with a sheet hot-glued around the cardboard to simulate a tablecloth. The sheet was bright orange, I might add—my worst color. Not that it mattered because most of my face was obscured by the fake fruit glued to the cardboard "plate." The result was beyond hideous. Plus, the costume was impossible to dance in. Pfft, *as if* anyone was asking.

My mind circles back to incidents like this when I wonder why I'm not married yet. It's simple math, really. If you subtracted all of the minutes and days and years I spent acting like a total spaz, my actual age in terms of social development is somewhere around twenty. Not nearly marrying age.

But if you think that a severed head was my worst Halloween debacle to date, you are wrong, my friend.

Last year, for example, I was Lil Wayne. Oh, it was a brilliant costume. I had a boyfriend at the time and took full advantage of the fact that he *had* to hang out with me, no matter how horrifying I looked. I wore XXL men's jeans, a white wife beater, a red Bedazzled Yankees cap over a dreadlock wig, and a grill on my teeth. I made my roommates draw every one of Weezy's many tattoos on my body and carried around a bottle of cough syrup and lollipops. I even talked in Wayne's gravelly high-pitched voice all night long. Only cops and black guys knew who I was supposed to be.

But it was the Halloween before that when my costume was the most memorable of them all, not for its creativity or oddness, but for the devastating effect it had on my social life.

It was just a few days before October 31, and none of my friends had come up with costumes yet. Still knee-deep in my emo revolution, I especially hated the idea of dressing in something frilly and sexy, so I suggested we go as a group of something. My top ideas were the Golden Girls, the Baseball Furies from *The Warriors*, the A-Team, or Pete Wentz.

"Wait, like we'd *all* be Pete Wentz?" asked Klo.

"Yeah, we could be a whole roving herd of Petes."

The girls stared at me and shook their heads.

"And you honestly wonder why you're single," said Pfeiffer.

Defeated, I spent the afternoon trolling around the picked-over costume store until I found four costumes so incredibly perfect I bought them all on the spot and rushed home.

"Teenage Mutant Ninja Turtles?" said Marcia, poking suspiciously at the outfits—green bodysuits, giant plastic shells, and nunchakus—as though they were cylinders of plutonium. "You realize these are children's costumes, right?"

The girls rejected the idea flat out, even when I volunteered to be the one carrying the box of pizza all night (authenticity is key). But I didn't care; I seized the Raphael costume and went to work. Since it was built for an eight-year-old, I cut a deep V in the bodysuit hoping that would give it some extra length. It didn't work and I was left with a raging camel toe that I tried to hide with a pair of beige boy shorts. Again, fail. I was beginning to think that this was my worst costume yet; at least the Merlin dress fit.

But I was out of time and had no choice but to follow through with Raphael, the "cool but rude" turtle, so said the package. Again, authenticity is key.

The girls scraped together some slutty, predictable costumes— Klo was a tarty maid, Marcia a naughty cop, and Pfeiffer (for the fourth year in a row) capitalized on her Sioux heritage and went as Pocahontas. They all looked adorable. I, on the other hand, looked like Quasimodo. As if my camel toe wasn't bad enough, the hulking plastic shell made it impossible to stand up straight.

We ended up at Fiddlesticks, a fratty bar in the West Village rife with fist-pumping ex–lacrosse players. I was in hell. Not that anyone noticed. I wrongly assumed that people would respect me for not dressing slutty. Maybe they did. I'll never know because no one would talk to me. Halloween is for sluts, pure and simple. It's the one holiday they have all to themselves. Patriots and hillbillies get the Fourth of July, drunks get St. Patrick's Day, the obese get Thanksgiving, and tramps dominate Halloween. I had gone against the natural order of things.

I ended up sitting alone in the corner, double-fisting Citron and sodas, and trying to chat up people in line for the bathroom. Once I realized I was making everyone uncomfortable, I tried to pretend that I was in fact a child who didn't know any better. That didn't work either—for some reason, talking in a baby voice asking, "Have you seen my mom?" wasn't endearing.

When the girls started complaining about the bar getting too crowded, I seized the opportunity to suggest we go to Pink Elephant, a new club that had just opened in the Meatpacking District.

Normally, attempting to get into a hot new club on one of the biggest party nights in the year would be an exercise in futility. But just prior to my emo overhaul, Klo and I had been total bottle rats. We partied at any and every club in the city, so I felt confident I could finagle our way in.

As we walked down the dank cobblestoned street, a trio of douchey guys sidled up alongside us.

"What's crack-a-lackin', ladies?" one said, smoothing his Christian Audigier shirt. "You headin' to Pink Elephant?"

Hoping that maybe they could get us in, I tried to flirt as best I could with nunchakus in my hand. But it became clear that these retards had no juice whatsoever, so we ditched them and put plan B into effect: lip gloss and schmoozing.

The key to getting into clubs is to be super-sweet, never pushy or entitled. Don't bother with lines like "You don't remember me?" No one remembers you, even if you fancy yourself a regular. The doorman have five hundred "friends" coming up to them all night expecting special treatment, so your best bet is to just ask politely what the crowd is like and wait for them to unclick the velvet rope.

But I didn't even get that far.

The bouncer, Sam or Sig or Sun—some single-syllable name not worth remembering—took one look at me and lost his fucking mind.

"You," he spat, pointing right at me, "I don't like your attitude." I looked over my shoulder, convinced he must be talking to one of the dozens of slutty nurses/stewardesses/bunnies lined up behind me. Then he turned his wrath on my friends and said, "All of you can just get the hell out of here because I'm not letting in anyone who's with that chick."

"Wait, what did she do?" asked Pfeiffer in protest as Klo, ever the diplomat, tried to smooth things over. "Okay, I think there's been an eensy-weensy misunderstanding," she cooed, batting her long eyelashes. "We're not with those other douches who just tried to get in. They've got Ed Hardy issues."

His eyes narrowed as he looked her up and down.

"Hmph. Fine," Sly/Stiff/Snake snorted. "You three can come in but not her—*everyone but the turtle*."

"But what did I do?!" I wailed, which of course made me look even more pathetic. Rule number two of clubgoing is never argue with the bouncer. Unlike with sex, "no" really does mean "no." But I'd had enough rejection for one night and wasn't about to take any guff from some ass clown in a fedora.

I was dragged away from the club by the girls, still hollering wretchedly that I was innocent. They had every right to ditch me, given that I was blubbering in a plastic children's costume, but they stuck by me. Fifteen miserable minutes later we walked into the only place in town where everyone really did know our name—Chelsea Square Diner.

The Greek manager immediately brought us the usual—a plate of cheese fries with Russian dressing—as we all sat down to eat our feelings.

I swore to hate Pink Elephant forever and even went so far as to steer clear of the Meatpacking for a good six weeks, lest I run into Slop/Snot/Snoop again.

But, because Jesus loves a good laugh, before my Meatpacking ban even ended, I spotted him at a holiday charity gala. I couldn't imagine that he remembered who I was—or cared—but of course I wouldn't be that lucky.

"Oh look," he sneered drunkenly, cornering me by the silent auction. "It's that fucking *turtle*."

I turned bright red. My poor date for the evening, Ben, a hulking banker Marcia had set me up with, was totally bewildered. The tale of dressing as a Teenage Mutant Ninja Turtle and getting blackballed from a club wasn't exactly a story I led with on dates, so I wasn't eager to explain.

"Um, I think you have me mixed up with someone else," I lied hopefully, but Snack/Snape/Snatch saw right through me.

"Pfft, *please*," he said, getting right up in my face, the stench of whiskey wafting off him. I hadn't noticed before but he was actually super-hot, wasteyface and all. "*I never forget an amphibian.*"

"All right, dude," Ben said, putting his massive hand on Sid/Slut/Spike's chest. "You're done here."

"I'm done here? *She's* done here! She's never getting into any club again *ever*!"

Before he could ball up his grapefruit-sized fist and shove it in Spud/Spit/Scum's face, I dragged Ben away and tried to explain. But the more I talked, the less sense I made. Camel toes, nunchakus, Ed Hardy, Pocahontas, Pink Elephants—it was more like a peyote hallucination than a story.

"So you really didn't do *anything*?" Ben asked.

I shook my head emphatically but I couldn't blame Ben for being skeptical—spend five minutes in my company and chances are I'll say something offensive. Factor in a goober of a costume and shots of tequila, and I was hard-pressed to come out smelling like a rose. Normally I don't really care if people like me or not, but Snorf/Smurf/Stench wasn't just anyone—he was a well-connected doorman capable of crushing the party-girl clout I'd worked years to amass. I *needed* him to like me, or I was facing a total social excommunication.

My chance for redemption came a month later, on New Year's Eve—or so I thought. Marcia and Pfeiffer and I had braved the bitter cold to trot to a house party thrown by our yacht-broker friend Grier. Every guy at the party was in Brooks Brothers and had some hideous girlfriend clinging to him, so the girls and I proceeded to drink our sexual frustration away. We were halfway through our fifth Coors Lights when someone in line for the bathroom caught my eye.

It was *him*, Sauce/Sav/Stump! I couldn't imagine who he knew in this stuffy, coupled-up crowd, but there he was, looking bored and lonely as he waited for the loo.

"Oh mah gahh, you guys," I slurred. "It's that dude who thinks I'm a turtle!"

The girls were convinced that this was fate pushing us together and that it'd make an absolutely adorable story for our grandchildren one day.

"It'll be jus' like *The Notebook*!" Marcia gurgled, opening a new box of wine.

"You haven't seen *The Notebook*, have you, Marcia?" asked Pfeiffer.

"I have not, no," she said. "But wha'eva, s'all the same—guy meets girl, guy calls her a turtle, and boom! They get married! Happens all the time."

"She's gotta good point, Pfeiffy. He and I are meant to be. Like Barack and Michelle."

They nodded in boozy agreement as I filled up my empty beer bottle with wine and toddled over.

"Heeyyyyyyy," I said, slinking up to him. "Happy new year. You gonna be nice this time?"

Slim/Stfu/Salt tilted his head slightly and considered his response. "Um . . . yes? Yes, I am going to be nice."

"Good baby," I cooed, stroking his lapel pervishly. "I think it's time we got better acquainted, ya know? I think it's destiny that you're here tonight."

He looked a little puzzled but broke into a smile and pulled me into the bathroom.

Within seconds he had me pressed up against the door in a passionate kiss, and I thought that maybe Marcia was right—all of our venom made for some sizzling chemistry. But I didn't want to give it all up, just enough to get him obsessed with me. With a little finesse, I could go from social pariah to Meatpacking Queen.

"I gotta go, lover," I said abruptly, pulling away.

"You're leaving?" he said, pouting.

"Yeah, but I'll see you Saturday night . . ."

I fully planned on finally hitting up Pink Elephant and using my newfound good graces to my advantage.

"How will I see you Saturday night?" he asked.

"Don't worry," I said, giving him one last kiss, "I'll come to you."

And with that I was out the door, staggering back to my friends just in time for the ball drop.

What a great start to the new year, I thought proudly. *Not only did I win over an enemy, I just might've started a new romance!*

For the next few days, I pictured myself suddenly becoming the darling of the New York club scene. Shrek/Stan/Swizz and I would become *the* It couple on the scene, velvet ropes parting for us all across Manhattan. I had already texted all of my friends announcing that I was once again flush with social currency and that Saturday night we were going big to Pink Elephant.

That night as I got ready and practiced my air-kiss in the mirror, I got a call from my friend Grier, who'd thrown the New Year's Eve party.

"Soooooooo," she said, "you made quite an impression on Nate the other night!"

"Oh, that's nice," I said uninterestedly. I figured he was one of the gawky guys I'd asked to open our fifth bottle of Charles Shaw. "Is he cute?"

Grier laughed. "Do you seriously not remember? Or did you just have your eyes shut that whole time in the bathroom!"

Wait.

"Bathroom?" I whispered, hoping against hope that this conversation was not going where I knew it was.

"Yeah, duh, Nate who you pulled into the bathroom! I think someone actually peed in my ficus because you guys were in there so—"

"*Who is Nate?*" I shrieked. "I mean what does he do for a living?"

Maybe I'd just misheard the bouncer's name on Halloween? "Nate" could be mistaken for "Snate," right?

"Well, right *now* he's a host at Outback," she said, quickly adding something about his awesome demo reel, but I'd already tuned out.

Was this really happening? Had I *seriously* hooked up with some loser restaurant employee for nothing?!

Humiliated, I sheepishly texted all of my friends and called off the celebration.

"But hey," I wrote miserably, "if anyone feels like a Bloomin' Onion at Outback, I've got a great hookup on a corner booth."

A Needle in a Ho Stack

There are some things in life that are worth making sacrifices for. My job as a gossip writer for the New York *Daily News* was not one of those things.

Snitching on the famous might sound easy, even fun. Stirring up trouble for the most ungrateful people on the planet? Why not! Screw 'em. And for a while, it *was* delightful. Our column brought in stories about celebs who cheated on their wives and did lines of cocaine off Brazilian hookers, and one hunky actor who bragged about giving girls herpes. I felt like the sword of justice, slicing through pretention and exposing the ugly, coked-up truth.

Then I realized that the people in my life had started to take a step backward. I had always been a vault of secrets, the one my friends came to for sound advice and discretion. And now here I was, mining every friendship I had for some kernel of gossip, and I hated it. But the pressure at work was unbearable. For a whopping $40,000 a year, I was expected to ruin the lives of celebrities. And in the process, I very nearly ruined my own.

Every day we gossips were expected to fill two enormous pages with scintillating tales, and most of the time, there just wasn't anything to write. Celebrities are either outrageously screwed up or mind-numbingly dull. Even if I did stumble across a juicy story, we usually couldn't print it for fear of getting sued. So we ended up trying in vain to make the most routine tidbit—Angelina avoids dairy! McDreamy buys paper towels!—seem interesting.

The real trouble started with the reality show. My editors had pitched a half-baked reality show idea—*Who Wants to Be a Gossip Columnist?!*—to a production company. But after interviewing me, the producers decided that my odd, awkward life was worth a closer look and my boss's concept didn't have legs. Over the next year, Crossroads Television and I developed a pitch and a pilot, and eventually landed ourselves a full-on TV series at MTV—*without* the *Daily News*.

But as my involvement in the world of television deepened, so did my bosses' resentment. Even though the network had no interest in including the newspaper in the show's plot, the paper started demanding royalties and executive producer credits, only to be laughed off by the production company. So if they couldn't squeeze money out of the show, they would squeeze misery out of me.

Boss A would routinely ask me to write stories or do interviews that would get me in trouble with the higher-ups, presumably with the intention of getting me fired, but who knows. Everyone who ran that place was so nutty I wouldn't be surprised if they were taking orders from a magical elf named Fiskers only they could see.

Boss B, meanwhile, made me feel like I was slowly losing my mind. One morning she made it clear that I was not to RSVP for events without asking permission first—I should wait until they were assigned to me.

Eight minutes later, she asked huffily why I didn't have any parties on the calendar.

"Uhhh, well, you said I can't RSVP to things, so . . . ?"

"*Shallon*. You need to be a little bit more proactive."

She said that a lot to me, and when she did, I would furrow my brow, nod resolutely, and begin opening and closing my file cabinets and shuffling papers randomly around my desk. There was no point in arguing. What would I say? "Leave me alone, I bring in great stories"? I didn't.

Maybe I wasn't the most "proactive" girl in the newsroom, but when Boss B said I had "no natural curiosity," well, that was just false. I am a *very* curious girl—just not about anything that mattered to them.

How many peanut butter cups can I eat before I feel nauseous and guilty? (eleven)

How long can I lurk outside my ex-boyfriend's building before the doorman gets antsy and calls the cops? (forty-five minutes)

Is red food coloring an acceptable substitute for cheek stain? (No)

"If your heart isn't in it, then why don't you just quit?" my friends asked me. Well, you see, rent cannot be paid with hugs and smiles, nor can health insurance premiums. And admittedly, there was a big part of me that wanted to stick it out. I wanted to be a writer, after all, and this was a good gig for a girl from Orange County.

But the worst was the managing editor, the Sea Hag. I called her that because I'm scared of the ocean, and I was scared of her. Also, the water holds all sorts of creepy, terrifying creatures who would gobble you up for no reason, as would she.

Sea Hag fancied herself the next Anna Wintour but really, she wasn't ruthless and brilliant, she was just a lonely old bully. It wouldn't take much to catch her evil eye. A grandmotherly German woman with too-strong perfume, the food blogger who once misspelled "brûlée," a features writer who had the gall to adopt a baby without the Sea Hag's permission—they all found themselves in her crosshairs. But she despised me most of all, and I had no idea why.

It was more than just a case of a manager being displeased with an employee—she hated me with the searing tenacity generally reserved for feuding teenage girls and Jihadists. If I was merely a failure as a reporter, why not just fire me? No no, the Sea Hag liked to keep me around to humiliate and berate in front of the rest of the staff.

I took the Sea Hag's abuse, for the most part, because I believed very strongly in the ethical goal of the paper, and even now I still do. While the management might have been a gaggle of demon harpies, the actual reporters and writers were brilliant. The paper consistently churns out fair and neutral stories, calls out corruption, and has a pretty kick-ass horoscope page too. Plus, unlike a lot of other New York–based tabloids, no one there ever seemed keen on *really* ruining anyone's life. Except for mine, of course.

Once the powers that be realized I was essentially useless as a reporter, they tried to figure out what niche I could fill. That niche, as it turned out, was hookers: when news broke of Eliot Spitzer's affair with a prostitute, I was the first person they turned to in hopes of identifying her.

Why they thought *I*, Idiot Employee of the Century, would somehow be able to triangulate which skank Spitzer nailed was beyond me. The only info we had on her at the time was that she was a brown-haired girl who went by Kristen.

"Well, Shallon," the Sea Hag asked expectantly, "who do you know?"

"Who do I know . . . that is a prostitute?"

She rolled her eyes.

"Uh, *yes*. You know, when we hired you, you presented us with this whooooole long list of sources and you need to pony up."

That list of sources was largely exaggerated, but even so I was pretty sure none of the people on the roster were hos or pimps. I thought about pointing this out, but my bosses had never labored under the oppressive umbrella of logic or fairness, so I just gritted my teeth and started to Google.

While my coworker culled every sleazeball source he knew, I signed up for a VIP membership to TheEroticReview.com so I could read evaluations of hookers and try to figure out who our Kristen was.

The irony was, I often compared my gossip job to prostitution. Going to parties, like sex, is great when you do it for fun, when you feel like it. But when you have to because someone is paying you, it becomes twisted and unbearable.

At least, that's how I'd always *thought* of prostitution. On the website, I braced myself for gross, misogynistic tales about guys making escorts wear the mask from *Scream*, or a saddle, or a bag over their head. I mean, isn't that why men see hookers—to play out the fantasies their wives or girlfriends would never allow?

No, actually. It sure wasn't.

I read comment after comment about guys who were just delighted that their girl allowed them to give her presents, massages, *oral sex*—things that seem to have been the pot at the end of the rainbow for "normal," non-sex-working women since the dawn of time.

I've been lonely since I broke up with my fiancée, but Ashleigh made me feel like a man again. I brought some oils and she let me

*rub her feet for awhile. I almost forgot about sex! She had to remind
me—I could've just rubbed her down for hours! —PoliSciProf*

In comparison, I once had a guy walk out on a date with me because I was left-handed and he thought that was "uncomfortably close to being handicapped." Then there was the guy who wrote:

*Julie has THE MOST perfect tits I've ever seen—I called down to
the concierge and had him send someone out to La Perla, this chick
needed to be dressed well. Def A+! —justme67*

My ex-boyfriend, on the other hand, got me a pair of onesie pajamas with feet last Christmas, but when I discovered that they were a little too short he said, "I don't think these were meant for someone as big as you." Another favorite was:

*Kassie showed up on time wearing a very sexy sweater dress that
really showed her beautiful body. We got to know each other for a
few minutes and retired to the bed for some snuggling and making
out. —panero_da_ghost*

Whereas last Halloween I dated a German guy with a goatee who wondered how girls felt when they kissed someone with facial hair. So, as a "joke," he bought me a fake mustache to wear one night while we hooked up. A Hitler mustache.

And of course, these whores also were getting a cool $800 for their 45 minutes of "work." I, on the other hand, worked incessantly—fourteen-hour days—at the expense of my integrity, for a mere pittance. I strutted around the city's dark, fetid streets like a ten-dollar whore, sacrificing way too much for way too little—a blind item here, a cheating rumor there—running furtively back to my bosses like they were some abusive pimp I was desperate to impress. The more I read Erotic Reviews, the harder it became to stomach the disparity between the hookers' lives and mine. I was young, educated, pretty, and accomplished . . . and couldn't keep a boyfriend to save my goddamned life. And yet somehow, there was a whole secret coven of these idiotic girls—failed actresses and models, waifish eastern European sluts with bad teeth, coke whores supporting a habit—and they were living my out *my* dream life.

How on earth was this possible? Were bubble baths and spooning *really* the clandestine desires Manhattan men were harboring? And willing to *pay* to actualize?!

I thought about my own sexual calamities—a banker who sweat so much in bed that I made him wear Under Armour; a waiter who suggested (unsuccessfully) that eight P.M. on Thursdays be "golden shower hour"; a guy we'll just call "Shave-y Davy"—and suddenly this whole hooker mystery made a lot more sense.

Men in New York have the luxury of living out their perverse fantasies every day, right out in the open. Girls here have learned to take what they can get. We are the true whores, not Kristen. We are the ones who lie down and take it, in the vain hope that love will be exchanged, instead of cash. And at the end of the night we'll blame it all on our madam, the city herself, who tells us that this is what New York is all about—excess and hedonism—and it's our job to put up with it.

Treating a woman well is the city's true underbelly.

Cómo Se Dice "I Wish I Was Dead"?

If it hadn't happened to me, I would have laughed.

It was eleven P.M. on February 13, the night before Valentine's Day, and I was getting dumped. Again.

Precisely one year before, my then-boyfriend Jack had pulled the plug on our four-month relationship, saying cryptically, "You're the only thing that makes me happy. I can't do this anymore."

Uh, what? Our relationship had been intense. We'd spent only three nights apart since the day we met and seemed to be heading in the "settling down" direction, which terrified and excited me all at the same time. Usually I managed to sabotage any relationship moving toward real commitment, but with Jack I wanted to make it work. Looking back, I'm really not sure why. The only place we really connected was the bedroom. Outside of those four walls Jack and I functioned like a brooding teenage boy and his obsequious mother.

I would rub his back and ask about his day and he'd roll his eyes, grumbling that I "wouldn't understand." Please. He was a writer for *The Onion*, not a triage surgeon.

But, like any fawning toady desperate to please, I kept trying. I brought him a T-shirt from my trip to the Super Bowl, only to later find it sopping up a puddle in his room. He told me my taste in music sucked, that I read stupid magazines, and that my optimism grated on his nerves—and I let him.

"I think he's jealous of you," Pfeiffer said one day, glancing pitifully at the unwanted cookies I'd baked him.

Jealous? Of what?

On paper, Jack was better than me in almost every way—he had a better education, made more money, had a bigger apartment in a cooler neighborhood. And yet, Pfeiffer was right; he resented me because I was inexplicably happier. I laughed easily and squealed over puppies and could derive immense pleasure from nothing more than a bag of candy and reruns of *Tool Academy*. But Jack, on the other hand, was a malcontent. In his eyes, the world had somehow wronged him, and no amount of Giants T-shirts or back rubs could ever make up for it.

But when the lights went out, we were unstoppable. The only problem with a relationship based on sex is that eventually you have to stop having it. You have to do things like eat and run errands, which can lead to conversing with the other person. And that really wasn't our strong suit.

I knew we were doomed the day my agent told me MTV wanted to film a pilot of my reality show. I called Jack, elated with the possibility of escaping my gossip job.

"If you do this," he said gravely, "I will lose all respect for you and never speak to you again, do you understand me?"

If this kid thought I was going to turn down my chance for fame in exchange for a lifetime of condescending snorts, he was dead fucking wrong. If I wanted out, this was my chance. But for some reason the thought of breaking up right then made me nauseous with misery. I just wasn't ready. I'm the kind of girl who has to learn things the hardest of hard ways. I give the people I love third, fourth, fiftieth chances.

I should have dumped you when I had the chance, I thought bitterly, months later, as I listened to him break up with me. I had put up with so much of his griping baloney, downplayed so many of my achievements to spare his ego, and for what? For *him* to leave me? On *Valentine's Day*? Really??

I called my levelheaded friend Danielle sobbing, looking for some translation of his "You're the only thing that makes me happy" line.

"It scares him that you're his foundation of happiness," she said patiently, "because he knows you're too good for him and will eventually move on."

Ah. A variation of the classic girl theory "He just likes you *too much.*" Pfft, right. How many times have my friends handed me that sack of hot crap? There are a lot of things I love too much— grilled cheese, underage lead singers, Coinstar machines—and the last thing I'm inclined to do is cut them out of my life. But for some reason, I'll buy into this wonky logic when it comes to boys. Like most girls, I'd much rather gag down a load of total BS than try to figure out and fix *my* shortcomings.

So there I was, alone and heartbroken on Valentine's Day 2008. And lucky me, a year later I got the chance to do it all over again!

Kyle was the exact opposite of Jack. He was young and buoyant and charming almost to the point of douchebaggery.

"You know, it's just a matter of time until you catch him wearing a Bedazzled Ed Hardy hoodie," Pfeiffy said, warning me. She was probably right, but I didn't care. I was just so thrilled to have a boyfriend who didn't outwardly despise me.

When I met Kyle, I had been dating a frenemy of his named

Ben. I adored Ben, but he also seemed to mostly hate having me around. But, unlike Jack, he didn't even want to get me naked all that often. Kyle heard rumors of my unhappiness and saw a golden opportunity to humiliate Ben *and* get laid.

In hindsight, this kind of malevolent multitasking should have been a red flag. But like I said, I felt lucky to date a guy who thought I was hot *and* cared whether or not I got sold into white slavery.

As pushy and neurotic as I am in most situations, I'm a very laissez-faire girlfriend. I have never asked any guy "Where is this going?" or tried to put a label on things. Well, at least not to his face anyway. Among my friends, any dude who so much as kisses me earns the label of "boyfriend." And if I'm drunk and there's some sneering girl sniffing around, he'll be described as my "very serious and rich fiancé . . . who has a yacht."

And what's the harm in that? No one has the right to interpret your situation for you. "Love," "boyfriend," "broken up"—these titles are just words, and totally subjective ones at that. One girl's booty call is another girl's satisfying relationship, and vice versa.

It was early December, and for our third date Kyle took me on a Christmassy tour of Manhattan. We put on ugly, snowmen sweaters and drank hot chocolate at a Christmas-themed bar he called the "reindeer barn." Under a bough of mistletoe, he suggested I meet his family.

"We're both from California," he said offhandedly, as if it were law that all California residents eventually meet each other's relatives. "And I want to get to know your mom too. But this will take our relationship from mellow to intense. Are you ready for that?"

I stared at him dimly. No one had ever asked me that before. My hands-off approach to my boyfriends tended to work a little too well. They generally made all the decisions (like when to stop calling) without ever bothering to inform me.

"Are you . . . trying to be funny? Is this a trick?"

He laughed, his green eyes sparkling. That was the thing with Kyle; nothing rattled him. Most New York guys would rather drink their own urine than say something *honest* and *vulnerable* to a woman. And if they did, and she responded with anything other than slobbering gratitude, he'd delete her number. But Kyle wasn't afraid to say anything. Not even on Valentine's Day. Not even, as I would discover, to break my heart.

The post-holiday deterioration of our relationship had been swift and confusing. We had met each other's parents, and as I watched him laugh and joke with his five siblings in their own warm, silly language, I fell totally in love with him *and* his large, boisterous Catholic family. As an only child, that kind of happy chaos was totally foreign to me, and it wasn't until I met his clan that I realized how much I longed for it. Maybe that played a role in our downfall—once you see how affectionate and giving a man can be, you start demanding that he treat you the same way, all the time. But I wasn't his family. I was just some girl he was dating, easily lost and overlooked in his family's bustling household.

Despite his theory that meeting the fam would make our romance more intense, things stayed very much the same. Maybe we just had different ideas of intensity. I took it to mean drive-through wedding chapels and matching tattoos. He was thinking more along the lines of posting pictures of us on Facebook.

It didn't help that I was severely stressed out at work. My bosses at the newspaper had turned hating me into an art form, and Kyle's analgesic optimism became the only bright spot in my life. At the end of my tether, I fell back on Kyle. I needed him to numb my reality, but no matter how much he gave me, it was never enough. I needed him to assuage every little insult or sideways glance I got on the job. But he was just one man up against a psychotic girlfriend and a whole corporation full of demons.

Suddenly, I understood Jack's abrupt departure. I had become the Jack in my relationship with Kyle—moody, selfish, and a real fucking downer.

Adding to the building tension, Kyle and I weren't sexually compatible. He got in the habit of coming over to my house wasted and passing out with his clothes on.

"You need to put out more," I finally said testily. "Or I'm going to start hooking up with other people."

"If you need something that I'm not giving you, you should totally go find it!"

This was not a wise thing to say to a girl who had a necklace that read "Revenge" custom-made . . . and wore it every day.

So I quickly rekindled a romance with Sterling, a gorgeous, self-obsessed banker I'd dated the year before. Any time we had plans I would drop hints to Kyle that I was going out with "a guy friend" and then would proceed to describe him in glowing terms.

"Cool!" Kyle said enthusiastically. "We should all hang out sometime!"

I gritted my teeth and tried harder. One night I purposely stole Sterling's boxer shorts and left them lying around for Kyle to find.

The next morning he just folded them up casually on his way out the door. "Oh, I put those boxers in your drawer, babe. Have a good day!"

Finally, a week before Valentine's Day, I sat Kyle down.

"Look, there's someone else who wants to take me out on the fourteenth, but I'd rather spend it with you. So you need to cowboy up or break this off."

Kyle thought about this and nodded slowly, saying nothing. Sterling, of course, had made no such request. But tools such as honesty weren't part of my romantic arsenal.

I wrongly believed that Kyle would take the bait and make some grandiose plan involving romance and champagne and roses, and I was giddy with anticipation when he came over the night before Valentine's Day . . . carrying a potted Peruvian lily.

"This is a birthday/friendship/Valentine's present . . . ," he said.

My face fell. "I'm sorry, did you say 'friendship' somewhere in there?"

"Shallon, look"—he fumbled with a petal—"I just can't give you what you want. I can't be that 'boyfriend guy' that you're expecting."

I felt like I'd been dipped in ice water.

"I'm *expecting* it, Kyle, because that's what *you promised me*. That's the kind of relationship your behavior, *your* actions, have led to."

Silence.

Getting dumped is like stubbing your toe. The real horror is the pain you know is just around the corner, the agony to come. I burst into tears, the floodgates crashing open spectacularly. I sobbed because I knew I had a long road of anguish waiting for me, weeks full of sleepless nights and depressing playlists. I managed to gurgle out that it wasn't supposed to happen like this—I should have been leaving *him*.

"Why would you leave me?" he asked simply, no trace of sarcasm or hubris in his voice.

"Because!" I wailed. "You're the only thing that makes me happy!"

"Aw, sweetheart . . . that doesn't make any sense," he whispered, rubbing my back, and I thought bitterly about just how wrong he was.

The next morning I woke up, puffy eyed and wretched, just as I had 365 mornings ago. I plodded into work with the faint hope that I wouldn't be assigned any events that night—very few celebrity parties took place on holidays. They, unlike me, had better things to do, with people who loved them. But leave it to the Sea Hag to whip up a hellish situation out of thin air.

"You're covering this. Tonight." She slapped a ticket down on my desk: *El Concierto del Amor con Marc Anthony y Jennnifer Lopez en Madison Square Garden!*

"There's a rumor they're splitting up and some people think they might announce it tonight at their concert," she said.

"Why would they announce their divorce at a *Valentine's Day* concert?" I mumbled. It would be like abandoning your child at the Olan Mills portrait studio.

"Look," she snorted, "just go, record everything they say, and file the story by midnight. Can you handle that, Shallon?"

"Do I get a plus-one?" Not like I had anyone to take, unless my body pillow counted. I could put it in a sweatshirt and spray it with Abercrombie cologne like I used to do in high school.

Sea Hag seemed to read my mind (or probably just my swollen, miserable face).

"*No.* The concert is sold out; we had to get this ticket on eBay for $250."

In a rare moment of fortitude, I decided to try to make the best of it. I had covered another J.Lo concert the year before in Atlantic City and had actually become a bit of a closeted fan. I inexplicably knew the words to every song, and while it wasn't something I admitted to at parties, I even liked *Gigli*.

In the off chance that J.Lo and Marc would address the crowd in Spanish, I arrived at the Garden early enough to pop into the Borders bookstore next door and pick up a Spanish phrase guide. Although it seemed unlikely that this pocket guide would contain such phrases as "legal separation" or "I just can't take her nagging anymore," an ace reporter is always prepared.

I had been to the Garden only for hockey games and Fall Out Boy concerts, both audiences I considered to be the fringe members of society, clearly making them "my people." But tonight MSG was packed with eighteen thousand Puerto Ricans festooned with flags, bandanas, and the ultimate Concierto del Amor accessory, a significant other. In other words, not "my people." I thought briefly about stopping to get a snack but I didn't want to stand out in any way, so I just merged into the crowd and drifted into the arena. Several times I called out a random gringo name—"Kevin! I'm back here, wait up!"—just to make it seem like I wasn't alone, that perhaps my non-fictitious boyfriend and I had gotten separated. This would have been more plausible if there had been one other white person at the concert besides myself.

I scooted past canoodling couples to my seat, my *one* seat, and tried to ignore the puzzled stares and whispers *en español*. I didn't even need the phrase book to figure out what they were saying— turns out "Is she here alone?" is universal in every language.

I flushed with embarrassment and poked the woman next to me, who was staring at her reflection in the glare of her boyfriend's gold medallions.

"I'm here for work!" I shouted above the din.

"Que?"

"I'm . . . I work for . . ." I groped, making swirly hand movements that were supposed to indicate writing but looked more like the foppish imitation of a flaming gay man.

She nudged her boyfriend nervously. "*Lesbiana,*" she said, shifting in her seat to get as far from me as possible.

Great. Not only was I alone but I also didn't even have any snacks. Then again, if I broke the seal of emotional eating, I might never stop. The janitorial crew would find me stuffed under the seats days later, smeared with congealed cheese, a stray hot dog bun sticking out of my bra.

At last, the lights went down and the audience erupted in cheers. At least in the dark I'd be less conspicuous, and who knows, maybe I'd bond with Jorge and Esmerelda in the seats behind me as we sang that our love don't cost a thing.

J.Lo and her husband came sweeping out onstage and launched into a Spanish ballad about escaping Nazi persecution . . . or something equally intense, judging by their dramatic choreography.

Okay, I'll recognize the next song, I thought, and I might have if I'd had the foresight to be born in San Juan or Aguadilla.

It slowly dawned on me that this concert was entirely in Spanish. There would be no discussion of which block Jenny was from, nor would anyone announce, "Let's get loud!"

After about five songs, Jennifer and Marc trotted their infant twins out onstage.

I whipped out my pen and paper, poised to capture a teary admission that yes, their odd marriage was over. Then maybe I'd have some purpose among the stadium full of weeping, devastated Latinos. I would make my way to the stage and seize the microphone and offer J.Lo tips on how make it through a mangled Valentine's Day. The Juans and Marias would cry out gratefully, "*La gringa es muy buena!*" and celebratory tequila would be passed forward in my honor.

But those hopes were dashed as Marc gushed that he and his

big-assed wife were happier than ever and the rumors of a split could not have been more false. As thousands of cheering fans hollered their support, I plopped down in my seat, dejected. Technically my assignment was over, and I could have left. But where would I go? My roommates were both out on dates. All that was waiting for me at home was Kyle's Peruvian lily, and it had begun to lean away from my incessant blubbering.

Yes, it was better to wait out the bulk of the evening in the dark shelter of Madison Square Garden. Sure, the people inside (correctly) thought I was a pathetic loser, but at least we probably didn't have many mutual Facebook friends. Out on the street, however, I stood a very good chance of running into a coupled-up friend out on a romantic stroll. Everyone thinks New York is a massive, sprawling metropolis, but in reality Manhattan is only a few square miles. You can't swing a dead cat without hitting someone you've slept with, and that night I wasn't going to take any chances.

So I huddled in my seat and tried to decipher the words to some of the more melancholy-sounding songs, scrawling unhelpful notes to myself—"sounds like 'Matterhorn'"—in hopes of translating the song later.

But as I sat there, watching the sea of couples swaying dreamily to the music, I realized the futility of my efforts. It would take more than a Spanish dictionary for me to ever fully understand the language of love.

Hoarders Without Borders

Working as a gossip writer for the New York *Daily News* was largely an exercise in masochism, but there were perks. Among them was the opportunity to make out with numerous celebrities—actors, musicians, athletes, you name it. But that wasn't even the best of it. Boys come and go. Gift bags, however (if you play your cards right), can clog up your apartment forever.

One of my chief duties as a gossip hack was to cover the Manhattan charity gala circuit. I loved going to these events, mostly because I ascended two social levels (in my mind, at least) every time I said the word "gala." *Gaaaaaala.* You really had to put your nose in the air and draw it out.

Charity functions are a lot like weddings: dressy people at huge circular tables eating and drinking and competing over who is better friends with the hosts. Only, instead of toasts and dancing, the entertainment mostly consists of "inspirational" presentations about why that particular nonprofit needs your money. Additional acts usually include a speech by some drunken old executive in the crowd whose wife goaded him into donating an obscene amount of money—one geezer gave $1 million at the last Christopher Reeve foundation dinner I attended—and then, of course, there was always the silent auction.

Sure, silent auctions are intended to raise money, but if you've ever been to one you know that all they really do is underscore how out-of-touch rich people are with how much things are worth. Five thousand dollars for a private cooking lesson with Mario Batali? Seven hundred dollars for a pair of Crocs worn by Plaxico Burress? Seriously?

"Who the hell would pay a grand for a bike signed by the Real Housewives of New Jersey?" Klo would ask. Whenever possible I would take her as my plus-one, but seats were usually tight to the best events, so she got stuck tagging along to parties that were about as fun as, say, the United Hispanic Volleyball Association dinner or a right-wing Abort Abortion bonanza.

As we listened to whichever D-list MC (usually a retired soap star or former Menudo singer) was hosting ramble about the majesty of giving, Klo would inevitably turn to me and hiss: "There'd better be a good gift bag, Lester."

Ah yes, the gift bag. The *true* reason anyone ever came to a benefit.

Bad gift bags are like boys with small penises—there's no way to predict the unpleasant surprise ahead of time. I can't tell you how many sacks I've greedily snapped up, only to find a heap of crap inside: combs, bird food, mints (oh, *so* many mints!), moisty-naps, XXL T-shirts advertising the services of Dr. Ira Weisenthal, DDS—the list goes on and on.

But when a swag bag is good, it's like Christmas morning. Flat-irons! Movie passes! Godiva chocolate! During the Super Bowl one year I snagged a $500 gift certificate to a spa in Santa Barbara. At the Denise Rich Angel Ball, everyone got Diptyque candles and Tempur-Pedic pillows. Hair products are also abundant on the Manhattan goody bag circuit, which is odd because most events are attended by old Jewish guys who don't have any hair (at least not on their head). Makeup is also really popular, most of which can be exchanged at Sephora with no problem, no matter where it's from. At one point, I had more than $1,200 worth of gift cards at the cosmetics store thanks to gift bag returns. I currently have enough lip gloss to choke a hippo.

But the gift bag cornucopia started coming to an end once my bosses at the *Daily News* realized that they hated me and began giving my buffoon of a coworker invites to the top-tier events, leaving me to cover Dog the Bounty Hunter's Flag Day Fiesta at the La Quinta Inn.

Since I knew there was no chance of getting any hot gossip at these phony-baloney benefits, I tried to guess the freebies ahead of time.

"So," I'd say casually to the publicist handling an event, "who all is sponsoring?"

She'd rattle off a few companies and I'd jot them down eagerly, quickly calculating the odds of decent loot.

It didn't take me long to figure out that sometimes, the worst events can have surprisingly fabulous gift bags. That's because the sponsors of those events tend to be new companies that are so eager to get their product in the hands of Manhattan's tastemakers that they'll practically give you the deed to their store. After the ill-conceived Alopecia Awareness Summit, for example, I was delighted to be gifted with a coupon for an entire year's worth of laundry service from an upstart dry cleaner.

But A-list sponsors tended to disappoint. My fellow reporters and I once daydreamed for weeks about the bounty that awaited us at a Cartier event . . . and were furious when all we pulled out of the swag bag was a jewelry-cleaning cloth and another goddamned box of mints.

Not long after that, I realized that I had no future as a gossip reporter (and didn't want one, either), so I took my lifetime supply of Altoids, peaced out of the *Daily News*, and started filming *Downtown Girls*. As demeaning and career-stifling as the place was, part of me—the greedy, cheap part—hated to leave the newspaper. Would I ever see the inside of the Plaza's ballroom again? Oh, how I love the Plaza! They could host a public execution and I'd be there with bells on as long as it was in that gorgeous, ornate ballroom!

After I quit, I sat in my bedroom and gathered all of the swag I'd amassed in those eighteen months around me, like children awaiting a story. I picked up each item—a bottle of Kiehl's shampoo, a Lia Sophia cuff—and kissed it, one by one. Would I ever again have the chance to add to this glorious collection of free stuff?

Turned out I need not have worried. Once word spread that I had my own MTV show, the gala invitations began rolling in. I again found myself rubbing elbows with socialites and celebs, and most important, gift bags. I still took Klo along with me because no one could work a room like the two of us. Within the first thirty seconds at an event, we'd have calculated where the hot single boys were clustered, which table would likely have an extra dessert, and which bartenders could be suckered into giving us a free bottle of Veuve Cliquot to take home. Plus—and this may sound stupid, but I assure you it isn't—Klo and I have complementary "good sides" when taking photos. I will be snapped only with my head turned to the right—if my chin is even one degree to the left, I look like a wheel of brie or a sweet potato. But Klo, the bitch, looks good from any angle, so she never has a problem letting me always be on the left.

We would drink, dance, and chat up people about our show, and usually I'd end up kissing some heir or another. But the best part of the evening was the cab ride home, when we'd giddily tear through our gift bags like kids on Halloween. Since she was engaged and I was atrociously single, I'd give her any men's products in exchange for something I wanted, usually candy, or hair products, which she doesn't use because she is naturally gorgeous. It was like having a diabetic friend who would trade you her Kit Kats for your boxes of raisins.

One evening, at the Bronx Zoo's Monkeying Around fund-raiser, I spotted something I wanted even more than the coupon for a free parakeet. His name was Xavier, and this gem of a boy was the son of a diplomat and currently in medical school at Columbia. We chatted all the way through the Cirque du Soleil performance and most of the live auction. He was tall and handsome and beyond dreamy, admitting that he went to these things only when his father couldn't and someone simply had to represent the family.

"Oh, I know exactly how that goes," I lied. When hobknobbing with socialites, I've found it's unwise to appear too different from them. They don't really value individuality or outsiders. They value being photographed, free stuff, and getting their name in the papers. Maybe we weren't so different after all.

"There *is* one event I begged my dad to get me into," he said conspiratorially. "The Doctors Without Borders gala. Are you going?"

The DWB benefit was one of the hottest events in town—*real* celebrities attended, like CNN anchors and congressmen. I would be hard-pressed to convince the event coordinators that I, future D-list reality star, needed to be there. But at that moment I decided I had to. Not only would the swag be out of control, Xavier wanted me to sit at his table. Eeee!

"*Kloey*," I said seriously in the cab home as we pawed through our loot, "I *have to go*. This guy could be my future husband!"

"You think everyone is your future husband."

The next day I got to work on my mission: get into the DWB event. I was too cheap to hire a publicist, so I used my Google Voice number to call event organizers and pretend to be my own rep.

"How y'all doin', this is Cindy Crosby," I trilled in a southern accent. "I'm tryin' to get my client on the list for next week's Doctors Without—"

"No can do," said the gay on the other end. "We're booked solid. Sorry!"

Furious, I hung up. I even called back, this time as actual Shallon, asking if I could cover it for my *Glamour* magazine blog.

"Hmm, nope," said the same gay. "We're all out of press tickets. You can cover the arrivals if you want."

I snorted. The *arrivals*? That meant lurking outside with a recorder, begging to speak to Manhattan's elite as they sauntered indifferently past. I'd rather eat my kitten.

I called Klo to whine and commiserate.

"Aw, that sucks you can't go!" she said sympathetically. "We would've all had so much fun!"

"Wait," I said, "who's 'we all'?"

"Well, Bob is going because one of his bands is—"

"*Are you kidding me right now, Klo?*" I fumed. "*You're* going and I'm not?!"

I begged and pleaded for her to let me tag along, but her fiancé, Bob, had barely been able to snag her a seat. Seething and bitter, I blamed Klo completely—I'd think of a reason to justify my rage later. *She* was supposed to be the one hoping to get an invite, not me. She was tall and pretty and stayed thin even though she ate like she was going to the electric chair. Being socially connected was the *one* thing I had on her and it was slipping through my fingers.

So rather than be the better person and help her pick a dress, I decided to take the low road and get revenge. Sure, I loved her like a sister, but if she was going to deprive me of a glamorous evening with Xavier and not even have the decency to feel bad about it, then I was going to find something to lord over her too.

Swag!

I vowed to amass as much free stuff as I could get my grubby little paws on and rub it all in her face. I would hit up every event this side of the Hudson River until I had a treasure trove of goody-bag loot that would turn her green with envy. But not just *any* loot— it would have to specifically be stuff that she needed and I didn't. Klo had four cats (I know, it's a miracle she's ever gotten laid, let alone engaged) and loved them like children. She was always volunteering at animal shelters and feeding strays. She even carries a baggie of kibble in her purse at all times in case a mangy kitten wanders into her path. Animals were her weakness and I was prepared to exploit it.

I scoured my list of upcoming parties but couldn't figure out which ones might have cat stuff in their giveaway bags. So I worked backward. I called the ASPCA, Petco, even Fancy Feast and Whiskas, staying on hold for hours in hopes of finding out if they were sponsoring any events in the near future. Oh, and they were—horrible, unbearable events. But I would go to every one: a cat spay-a-thon in Yonkers? Weehawken's third annual Guinea Pig Fashion Show? The Meow Mix make-your-own-litter party at a homeless shelter? Bring 'em on! Laughing like a madman, I triumphantly RSVP'd for each wretched fund-raiser I could find, as long as it had an animal theme. And of course, I made sure she knew about it.

"You bitch," she growled into the phone when I called her from the Your Dog Can Draw! party in Staten Island. It had taken me almost two hours to get there, but I didn't care.

"Sorry, Kloey, I can't hear you over all of these *adorable* barking puppies!" I laughed cruelly as she hung up on me. They say that when you pursue revenge you dig two graves—one for your enemy and one for yourself. I couldn't speak to the grave thing, but digging certainly seemed correct. I had accumulated so much useless swag in my studio apartment that I could barely get to the bathroom. Each morning required at least fifteen minutes of excavation and re-arranging just to reach my coat closest, and don't even ask what all I'd stuffed into the storage ottoman. With the trillions of condoms I had already squirreled away under my bed, I really didn't have room for yet another hoarding obsession. I'd even converted the oven into cargo space, jamming it full of newly acquired men's grooming products that I now refused to give my best friend.

But Klo was a worthy adversary.

"Oh, sorry," she said when I arrived at her apartment for our weekly sushi and T.J. Maxx shopping date. "Just shove all that stuff out of the way."

It's not easy to make her two-story penthouse apartment look cluttered, but everywhere I turned, I was tripping over a swag bag.

"Is this . . . a case of Butterfingers?" I said incredulously. I *loved* Butterfingers. "And Reese's Peanut Butter Cups?!"

"Mmm-hmm." She smiled, clearly enjoying my brewing tantrum.

"But you're allergic to nuts!" I yelped. "These should be mine!"

"Well, you're allergic to cats, but that hasn't stopped you from stockpiling cat food, now, has it?"

I scowled. I knew we should quit this arms race but I wasn't ready to capitulate just yet. That's when Klo upped the ante.

"Wanna go dress shopping with me?" she said casually over lunch. "I need something stunning for Saturday."

I narrowed my eyes. I could smell a scheme.

"What's Saturday?"

"Oh, ya know," she said, tossing her long, dark hair breezily, "just the Rangers' Casino Night at the Plaza."

I made a sound that was somewhere between a shrieking goat and a car backfiring. Hockey? At the Plaza?!

"You . . . you can't be serious," I whispered furiously. Monopolizing gift bags was one thing, but going to a party stuffed to the gills with beefy, delicious hockey players was a blitzkrieg attack. I could hog all the cat events I wanted; she still had four at home to play with. But try as I might, I couldn't find one single NHL star lurking underneath my couch.

"All right, you win," I announced. "You don't play fair, but you win."

"I know." She grinned triumphantly. "That's why I always win!"

That night I turned over all my kitty paraphernalia and men's toiletries and she in turn sent me home with a stack of peanut butter candies and even some Blonde Ambition shampoo that she'd been hiding.

I never did get to go to the Doctors Without Borders benefit, nor did I ever see future-husband Xavier again. But I did learn a few things from my brief cold war with Klo: One is that Bedazzling pooper-scoopers does not a party game make (animal charities, please take note). And two, if you're going to mess with my best friend, do it in a city without an NHL team.

I Brake for Preppies

My hometown of Irvine, California, is the epitome of suburbia. Nicknamed "the Bubble," Irvine is a shining example of uninspired urban planning. Each perfectly paved road leads to a mini-mall. Every lawn, tree, and park is impeccably maintained and manicured because it's the law. The homeowners' associations decide what color you can paint your house and what kind of front door you can have, and absolutely forbid incendiary propaganda like a VOTE MARGIE FOR PTA PRESIDENT! sign on your lawn.

There isn't litter or graffiti or homelessness or black people. Instead, there are golden retrievers. Tennis clubs. Swimming pools. Manmade lakes kept at the ideal shade of blue and culs-de-sac brimming with happy, serene, upper-middle-class families.

The rarely used police have an adorable definition of crime and fill the blotter with calamities like THIEF MAKES OFF WITH BOTTLE OF DETERGENT AND FABRIC SOFTENER FROM ALBERTSON'S BEFORE FLEEING IN A MERCEDES and $10 IN CHANGE LIFTED FROM AN UNLOCKED CAR; IPOD AND CDS LEFT UNTOUCHED.

Growing up there, I had always self-identified as a preppy. After all, if Irvine wasn't straight out of the pages of *The Official Preppy Handbook*, what was?

But despite my perfectly perfect town, my own homelife was rather alternative. Before having me, Mama had been like pre–Brad Pitt Angelina Jolie—globe-trotting, wild, man-eating, and fiercely independent. But like Brangelina, parenthood had mellowed her, so she moved to Irvine for the first-class school system. Still, she never could fully succumb to the banality of suburban life. When I was little, before she became a nurse, she worked as a flight attendant. So while most Irvine moms were carpooling to soccer practice, she was off chasing Parisian sunsets. My overprotective great-grandmother took care of me while Mama was away and would do things like pack turnips in my lunch box and lecture my friends on why poking too much at their belly buttons could kill them.

When Mama was home, we'd engage in all manner of subversive, bohemian activities, like visiting Buddhist temples and seeing jazz shows.

We didn't even vacation like normal people. Because my mom flew outside the continental U.S. for free, I had visited more third-world countries than I had American states by the time I hit puberty. While other kids were lounging poolside in Palm Springs or Hawaii, I was gagging down malaria pills and trekking around Ecuador, Kenya, Bali, Egypt, Tanzania, the Amazon, and God knows where else. In a lot of ways, it made me compassionate and streetwise. But those traits took a while to ripen. At the time, it just made me skittish and Pavlovian—I associated packing a suitcase with nonpotable water and government coups.

Sure, our trips were exciting, but secretly, I longed for a normal, boring life. I wanted PTA meetings and minivans, not safaris and shawarma. As a teenager I had no real need for rebellion. Why bother being *more* alternative? I was already the girl with the jet-setting mother, no father, and an unnatural obsession with her cocker spaniel.

So, desperate to blend in, I dressed exclusively in pleated shorts, pastel, and anything caught standing still at the Gap. This dovetailed right into a worrisome Republican phase during junior high—my own personal brand of disobedience—which had my staunchly Democratic family more than a little concerned.

But still, my mom was determined to punk me up, so she took me to visit my godmother, Toni, in San Francisco. Toni announced that I was "square" and dragged me around the city, regaling me with tales of my mom and her as freewheelin' hippie chicks lookin' for "ass, grass, or gas."

"You were looking for gas?" I asked. "What does that even mean?"

"It's just an *expression.*" She sighed with exasperation. "C'mon, sister, we need to get you *hip!*"

Toni and Mama were delighted to prowl Mill Valley's weed-scented record stores and sip espresso at coffeehouses staffed by real live lesbians, but I, on the other hand, was terrified. I waited in the car with my Rush Limbaugh autobiography.

Sure, San Francisco wasn't exactly Beirut, but to me the alternative lifestyle I witnessed there was more disturbing than anything I saw abroad, precisely because it *wasn't* abroad—it was *here.* Within driving distance of *my home.* I had no problem roaming the streets of Egypt after dusk or hitchhiking around Northern Ireland. But in California, the only place I felt safe was Irvine.

This provincial attitude displeased Mama greatly. So in tenth grade, just before the Woodstock-themed Sadie Hawkins dance, she decided to take matters into her own hands—and closet.

"Let me just *try* dressing you up for the dance," she said enticingly. "I have a shirt that would be perfect!"

Now, despite being conservative and dorky, I had fallen in with the popular crowd, an enclave of rich, WASPy prepster kids with fleets of Suburbans and summer homes in Tahoe. They all knew each other from kindergarten, and I was one of the few "outsiders" to infiltrate their clique. This dance would be one of my first outings with the Preppy Spice kids (as my artsy friend Ellen called them), and I wanted to impress. Nonetheless, I relented and let my mom dress me; I was hoping I'd win some street cred by wearing clothes that were *actually from* the sixties.

Let me just say up front that as a fifteen-year-old student council nerd who'd never kissed anyone, I had no idea what a quaalude was. So I couldn't possibly foresee the controversy of wearing my mom's "Quaalude Queen" T-shirt to the dance. Given that the Preppy Spice kids were just as straight-edged—after homecoming we made s'mores and played spin the bottle—they didn't know what a quaalude was, either. But my math teacher sure did. Same with Vice Principal Butell, Coach Cunningham, and Señora Sorey.

"Either the shirt goes or you do," Coach Cunningham said, glowering, so I spent the rest of the dance in a dusty, XXL "UHS Trojan Football" T-shirt he dug out of his office.

Seething, I called my mom and bitched her out. She thought it was hilarious.

"Honey, this is great!" she cackled on the other end. "You'll be the coolest girl in school!"

"*Wrong,*" I hissed, "the coolest girl in school is Elizabeth Link, and she's a debutante who plays soccer and wears ribbons in her hair. *Not T-shirts condoning drug use, Mom.*"

Much to my ire, Mama was right—the whole school was buzzing over my quaalude kerfuffle, turning me into a minor celebrity. I began to think that I actually had a shot at ascending the Preppy Spice popularity ladder, and by senior year, I was on prom court and led the student council. Ellen even had an I BRAKE FOR PREPPIES bumper sticker made to commemorate my social victory. I had done it: I had conquered the preps. Not many teenagers can credit quaaludes with helping them dominate high school. At long last, I was ready for a big heaping helping of nonconformity. College was going to be a festival of weird, a myriad of alt-experiences! Ass, grass, or gas!

And it was . . . for lots of other people. Not me. Nestled in the Northern California countryside, Cal Poly wasn't exactly a mecca for the unconventional. I'd never seen so many white people in my life. Cowboy hats, Wranglers, and F150s were as ubiquitous at Poly as herpes was at UC Santa Barbara, two hours away.

Okay, I thought, starting to twitch at the thought of *four more years* spent in neutral colors and silver Tiffany jewelry, *I can do this. I triumphed over Preppy Spice, I can triumph over Cal Poly!*

But I didn't want to. I wanted to take pills and pierce things and stay out all night and date dangerous boys! And it wasn't going to happen, at least not yet. I kicked myself for not taking my mom's advice and rebelling when I was younger.

So, six years later, after Alex plunged me into a black abyss of depression that sparked my emo revolution, part of me was secretly happy. At long, long last, I could seize dysfunction by the horns and dive headlong into self-destruction.

But after a year and a half of punk shows, black nails, and East Village dive bars, I was getting sick and tired of being sick and tired. Hoodies and skinny jeans were pretty uncomfortable during a sticky Manhattan summer, and guys never wanted to invite the brooding twenty-five-year-old in a My Chemical Romance shirt out to their

Hamptons house. And I was over hooking up with wee little emo boys who weighed less than I did—it was like having a lesbian experience. I was ready to date men again—real *men*.

So when my friend Livingston—"Liv" for short—invited me to her parents' beach house in Martha's Vineyard for the Fourth of July, I took it as a sign from God that it was time to return to my preppy roots.

Despite her blue-blood name—Livingston Howland Potter— she and I had met in the least-upper-crust way possible: over the Internet. She had been an Ice Girl (a hockey cheerleader, basically) for the Boston Bruins and had stumbled across my hockey-centric blog one day.

We began corresponding and, each reasonably certain that the other was sane, met up at her place in Boston when I was there hosting a party for Trojan.

"This weekend is going to be *so* fun," she told me. "Our house is actually on Chappaquiddick, but we go to Edgartown on the Vineyard at night to drink. You'll absolutely die when you see all the guys in Nantucket Reds!"

I nodded eagerly but had no idea what she was talking about. Nantucket Reds? I hoped it was a hockey team.

"You don't know what Nanny Reds are?" my roommate Marcia laughed. "Honey, you've been in emo town too long! You need a crash course in prepster."

"Pffft, I do not," I said, scoffing. "I grew up preppy."

Pfeiffer and Marcia smirked.

"East Coast preppy is very different than West Coast preppy," Pfeiffer explained. "Like, what do you know about boat shoes and needlepoint belts?"

I stared at her blankly. I knew each of those words individually—

"boat," "shoes," "needlepoint," "belts"—but as conjunctive items? No clue.

While I had been knee-deep in Warped Tour this and guyliner that, my roommates had been enjoying a preppy renaissance. They turned to Facebook to illustrate just how much I had to learn.

"Okay," Pfeiffer said, pulling up a picture of her friend Reyn— short for Reynolds, naturally—in a typically preppy outfit. "Notice the Nanny Red lobster pants and the—"

"Wait, lobster pants?"

"Yeah, they have little lobsters embroidered on them."

I wrinkled my nose. "Why?"

"You know how black people wear shirts for the teams they like? Well, preppies wear clothes advertising what they like about the ocean—lobsters, sailboats, whales, et cetera."

"This is a joke, right?"

"No," Marcia said, "and trust me, you *will* be tempted to laugh at them, but just try to keep in mind that they're worth jillions of dollars."

As I looked at pic after pic of shaggy-haired guys in blue blazers and lank girls in pink and green dresses, I started to panic. This type of prepster was completely foreign to me. This had to be some sort of hoax.

"Yeah, but I strongly doubt Liv's family is like this," I said nervously. "Her brother Tripp just graduated from Texas, so—"

"Wait, her brother's name is *Tripp*?" Marcia giggled.

"Yeah, I don't know what it's short for. Maybe Tripton or something?"

"Um, no, Shallon." Marcia bit back a laugh. "It means he's a third. Like, Something Something Potter the third—Tripp as in *triple*."

Oh dear. "So then his best friend Quattro would be . . . ?"

"A fourth."

Oh. Dear. It was becoming clear that my transition back into preppiness would not be a smooth one. Frantic, I called Klo for help.

"Well clearly, you need to lie," she said. "Just use my life as a template—say you went to the same boarding school that I did, and I'll even give you some of my old Deerfield sweatshirts, and I have some embroidered belts too!"

But since I couldn't exactly pair a whale belt with ripped, acid-washed skinny jeans, Klo and I headed to Bloomingdale's.

"This is Lilly Pulitzer!" she said, waving her arm triumphantly over a hideous collection of dresses so garish and bright it was giving me a migraine. And even worse, *everything* was knee length. My style had devolved into two settings: emo and slutty. These contraptions were neither and I hated it.

I tugged a dress's oppressively high collar. "I feel like it's choking me!"

"It is." Klo smirked. "It's choking the hipster slut right out of you, Shallon."

But I refused to spend three hundred dollars on something so stiff and unflattering, so I arrived at the Vineyard with a suitcase full of tatty boho dresses from three summers ago. They couldn't be *that* out of style, right? Besides, Liv had never struck me as particularly Pulitzer-ian when we'd hung out before. So imagine my surprise when she picked me up from the island's tiny airport in a pink polo and madras skirt. I, on the other hand, was wearing faux-leather leggings and a tank top with a skull on it. I looked like the town's executioner.

I instantly regretted not getting the Lilly dress and realized that the last-minute trip I'd made to J.Crew wasn't going to do much good. One pair of pink flip-flops wasn't going to impress these people.

"Oh, don't worry!" she said, reading my mind. "Our family really isn't *that* preppy."

I suspected that she was lying through her perfect teeth, but I gave her a grateful smile anyway. I heaved my suitcase into her trunk and noticed the license plate said CHPQDCK. *Chappaquiddick*. Not that preppy, eh? I was so screwed.

As we drove through the lush, verdant island, Liv tried again to downplay her family's blue-bloodedness.

"Our house is seriously just a shack," she explained. "Honestly, it's nothing fancy; we're going to just tear it down one day and totally start from scratch."

"Shack" was not an accurate description of their beach house mansion. Perched on a cliff overlooking the quaint Edgartown harbor, their charming home was right out of a Nicholas Sparks novel. It was rustic and littered with sailing trophies, black and white photos of tight-lipped New Englanders, and nautical tchotchkes. It was like an architectural version of your favorite well-loved stuffed animal. I adored it.

Stairs led down from the main house to the boathouse and dock, where their two boats—a Parker and a Regulator, I learned—bobbed in the water.

"Dad and Tripp are out sailing, but *hiiiii!*" Liv's mother came skittering into the living room with tight, warm hugs for everyone. I adored her too. Lissie Potter reminded me of Kelly Ripa—small, blond, bubbly, and yet commanding respect and just a little fear. She was wearing an orange and white Lilly dress that I had definitely tried on and definitely *definitely* hated. It had made me look like a creamsicle on acid, but she looked marvelous. I could never imagine my mom in such a garment. Her favorite outfit was a silk romper from Bali that she paired with carved African bracelets and custom-made sandals from Capri.

Liv's friends Kayla and Laura arrived a few hours later, and I immediately latched on to Laura because she was black and I assumed she would also feel out of place. Wrong again, Lester. Laura was the preppiest of us all, refusing to wear shorts more than three inches above the knee because they're "terribly inappropriate."

We spent the weekend lazing around at the Chappy Beach Club, a treasure trove of WASPy tittle-tattle, listening to Lissie point out who was sleeping with their babysitter and who was addicted to Xanax.

The other girls nodded vaguely, much more interested in soaking up sun than gossip, but I hung on every salacious word. If I was going to leave emo boys behind for good, I was going to need a preppy mentor, and Lissie was it. I begged her to teach me how to snag my very own trust-funder.

"I just don't think I *look* like the kind of girls they usually date."

Lissie waved off my worry with her bejeweled hand. "Honey, you're on TV, remember? Celebrity goes with everything. You go, girl!"

Obviously, she was defining "celebrity" pretty loosely. At the time, I'd just finished filming the show, and no one had any reason to know/care who I was. But she was onto something. I should play to my strengths. I was never going to be the perfectly proper New England girl. Not without lots of Ativan, anyway. I was too bold, too brassy, too large of a presence. I decided to try to use this to my advantage.

Later that day was the annual Fourth of July flotilla—which I'd been mispronouncing as "flow-tee-ya" (thanks, Mexican food)—an event in which all the Vineyard's young people sail out to Cape Poge and tie their boats together for a massive on-deck party. I put on a giant floppy hat and Prada sunglasses and practiced saying "No photos, please" in the mirror. With any luck, I could convince people that I was Lauren Conrad.

We motored up to the flotilla, already half-drunk on coconut water and rum, and one boy immediately caught my eye.

He was tall, broad shouldered, and pale with curly blond hair.

"He was a *ginger*," Klo would later insist, shuddering with revulsion. But she's a brunette and they're too busy waxing their mustaches to understand the complex subtleties of blondness.

Whatever he was, I was intrigued. Oddly, it was his swimming trunks that caught my eye. They were neon green and looked a little like boxers—a far cry from the knee-length board shorts those California boys wore. With his nose stripe of zinc oxide and pink Wayfarer sunglasses, he looked like the jock from an eighties movie.

The shorts, Liv explained, were something called Vilebrequin, and the boy was someone called Wickham Brooks.

All my synapses fired at once. *Wickham Brooks.* I was sold on the name alone. Liv filled me in on his pedigree: grew up in Connecticut, went to some East Coast college where people wore blazers to the dining hall, worked as a hedge-funder in Manhattan. And he had two siblings, which meant that he was *literally* a Brooks brother.

I needed a closer look. I hopped gingerly across the boats to his vessel, where he was fist-pumping to "Danger Zone."

Celebrity, celebrity, celebrity, I repeated to myself.

"Hey there," I said demurely. "Do you have any ice? Our bottles of Cristal are getting hot."

Wickham, still fist-pumping, got right up in my face. For a second, I thought he was going to kiss me.

"GONNA TAKE IT RIGHT INTO THE *DANGER ZONE!*" he belted at the top of his lungs, and head-banged away into a group of girls in Ralph Lauren one-pieces.

I sulked all the way back to our boat; was this guy seriously choosing a cluster of Merediths over *me*? I balled up my little fists like a villain in a Lifetime TV movie.

"You *will* be mine, Wickham!"

My second chance came a few hours later as we sailed back to Chappaquiddick and noticed two guys stranded in the middle of the ocean, floating on a small capsized sailboat. Everyone was too drunk to care and sailed on, until I realized one of the shipwrecked sailors was wearing neon green swim trunks.

"Tripp, turn the boat around," I said. "My future husband is floating out to sea!"

Brilliant, I thought with a scheming smile. *I'll save his life and he'll thank me by proposing.*

"Oh my goodness, are you all right?!" I said dramatically as we motored up, fighting the urge to add *Yes, it's me, Shallon Lester, star of MTV's hit* Downtown Girls, *to the rescue!*

Clinging languidly to the boat's broken sail, neither of them seemed too concerned about being stranded in the Atlantic; Wickham was sipping a Smirnoff Ice while his friend took a final swig of his Bud Light and tossed the empty into the waves.

"Do you guys have any more beer?" the friend asked.

"Oh yes," I said. "All the beer you want . . . up here in the boat! The nice dry boat!"

I felt like the White Witch coaxing Edmund into her sleigh with Turkish delight. After a few minutes of cajoling, I finally convinced them to come aboard, where I attempted to make small talk with Wickham. Wasted and waterlogged, he wasn't much of a conversationalist. But he *was* decidedly uninterested in me, which was all I needed to become totally obsessed with him.

"They'll be out later tonight," Liv said, trying to reassure me, as we dropped them off in Edgartown. "But *uck*, I don't know why you like him; he was such a little shit when he was younger. I can't imagine he's changed."

I thought about what my friend Ellen had pointed out one time: I don't date people, I date *types*.

"You say 'I want a preppy, I want an athlete,'" she explained. "But you never say 'I want someone smart, I want someone funny.' It's like you're shopping instead of dating—*I'm running out for eggs, milk, a Rockefeller, and a pro lacrosse player*."

But my checklist methodology made dating easier, especially in New York. It helped you decide how to dress and where to go— Upper East Side for preps, SoHo for Eurotrash, East Village for unemployed musicians. Even back in high school I'd been a social chameleon, building sets with the theater dorks one day and sharing a limo to prom with Preppy Spice the next.

What else was I supposed to do? Judge someone based on their *personality*? Sweet cracker sandwich, I don't have all day! Imagine the effort that goes into talking to every boy one meets without these categories as filters. The thought alone exhausted me. Besides, boys were always typecasting girls—blondes over brunettes (obviously), Jews over gentiles, tits over ass. If they could do it, why couldn't I?

That night we ran into Wick at the Atlantic, a local bar stuffed to the gills with prepsters. He was clearly well on the road to blackoutville, careening around the dance floor like a heat-seeking missile, before landing at Laura.

"You . . . you wanna make out?" he slurred.

"Uh, *no*," she said, adjusting the pink ribbon in her hair.

Wick didn't really take no for an answer. He grabbed Laura by the ears and made out with her face; I don't know if you could really call it kissing, but it did involve lips, tongue, and spit.

She pushed him away and he toddled off as I burned with jealousy. But oh, my turn for some oral assault would come soon enough. After last call, everyone spilled out into the street and Wickham wandered up to us.

"I remember you," I said coyly. "I fished you out of the ocean this afternoon."

Before I knew it, his tongue was in my mouth and Liv was whipping out her camera to capture it. And then, just as quickly, he disengaged and was be-bopping down the street.

I wiped the slobber off my mouth and smiled, predatory schemes unfolding in my head. *Oh yes, Wickham . . . you will be mine.*

Phase the First being complete, once I got back to the city, I took the next logical step—stalk the bejesus out of him on Facebook. I refused to friend him right away, but he was dumb enough to leave numerous photo albums public, so my roommates and I spent that week doing research.

It became clear he wasn't just *a* preppy, his blood was bluer than the man-made lakes of my Irvine youth. Every picture featured a sailboat, Nantucket Reds, guys who looked like Kennedys, or all of the above.

"Well, he's no Lord Voldemort, that's for sure," Marcia said, clicking through his "Sailing to the Caymans" album.

"Meaning that he's taller than five-foot-three and doesn't look like a white version of Prince?" Pfeiffer quipped.

"I dunno," Marcia said, squinting at a photo of Wickham and his dad in Antarctica next to their boat. "He's just so . . . *different* from everyone you've dated."

Exactly. Dating emo guys had yielded one disaster after the next, culminating with the Voldemort nuclear holocaust. I couldn't go through that again, not ever. I needed a boy with no possible chance of getting to the real me, and Wickham was it. Wick seemed dull, immature, and two-dimensional—perfect for my fragile heart.

A few days later I put Phase the Second into action: I friended him on Fbook, adding a note: *I know you . . . you Frenched my friend and me over the 4th in the Vineyard. Classy!*

Within two hours, he'd accepted my friend request and sent me a message apologizing for the face rape. Before long, we were messaging back and forth every hour. By sunset, he had asked me out for drinks.

Phase the Second: complete. I tried my hardest to craft a modest, New England–appropriate outfit, I really did. But I just can't resist dressing like a tart, so I turned up in a short skirt and heels.

I fully expected Wickham to be dreadful, but since I'd already named our future sons—Sebastian and Bridger—I downed a shot before leaving the house and hoped for the best. All I needed was a guy I could tolerate and parade around as my preppy trophy boyfriend. Nothing more, nothing less.

Really, I can't tell you how disappointed I was to find Wick to be charming, smart, witty, and incredibly sexy. We talked for hours and kissed in the cab home; it took every ounce of my self-control not to drag him up to my bedroom, but I didn't. The next morning, he texted me to say that he'd had a wonderful time and couldn't wait to see me again, and before I knew it, we'd set up a dinner date for Friday night. Pfft, *great*. This was the last goddamn thing I needed—an actual, nerve-wracking, tummy-fluttering crush.

"Please, *please* don't send him a creepy text like you always do," Marcia begged. "He sounds rich and I feel like his apartment building has a pool and I'd really like that this summer."

"Yeah, remember that time you texted that guy Steve '*I can't stop smelling my fingers*' after you ate barbecue at Brother Jimmy's?" Pfeiffer hollered from the kitchen. "And then you were like, 'Wahh, I don't understand what happened?!'"

As my roommates howled with laughter, I decided against telling them that I'd *already* sent Wickham a creepy text. It just sort of . . . slipped out. During our date, he had told me all about his sailing adventure to Antarctica and we'd made a joke about polar bears and how he kind of looks like one. So naturally, thinking it'd be *soooo* cute, I had texted "*Looking forward to dinner with a polar bear tomorrow night. I'll bring some raw fish for you to catch in your big ol' paws.*"

Apparently he didn't remember our bear talk one bit because he replied with "*???*" and I was sure I'd flushed my chances down the drain. I wrote back "*Oh sorry, totally sent that to the wrong person! You're next to my friend Wendy in my phone!*"

As if that's less creepy, Shallon. I suddenly dreaded our date. That idiotic text had drained me of any power or upper hand. He probably had the Ick so badly, and if he didn't, I was sure he would once he got to know me. How could I relate to his world of polo ponies and country clubs when I'd only recently learned that Martha's Vineyard *wasn't* owned by Martha Stewart?

And then, just a few hours before our date, Jesus bestowed a miracle upon me: a sprained ankle.

I was kickboxing with my trainer, Reggie Chambers, when I rolled my ankle and had to get crutches. Even as I writhed in pain on the floor of the gym, I celebrated my stroke of luck. Injuries are a girl's best friend when it comes to dating, and I hobbled home with a smile on my face; this orthopedic boot would put Wickham right where I wanted him.

I crutched into the restaurant like a wounded bird as Wickham leapt up in alarm.

"Shallon! What happened, are you okay?!" His face filled with chivalrous concern.

"Oh," I said meekly, wobbling for effect, "I'm fine, don't worry about me. How are *you*?"

He fussed over me the entire night, sitting on the same side of the booth and cracking my crab claws for me. The polar bear text debacle had been totally eclipsed by my fabulous new malady, but now a new problem was looming on the horizon: connection. True, real, person-to-person *connection*. Maybe my being physically vulnerable made him want to open up emotionally, but whatever the impetus, he and I talked for hours, about everything. Parents, dogs, work, guns, college, politics, oysters—everything.

That night when I got home I floated (as much as one can float on crutches) through the door, gushing details to Pfeiff and Marcia.

"I think I actually like him for *him*, not just the preppiness anymore."

The girls looked worried.

"Just be careful, Shallie," Marcia said. "Preppy guys are like Jewish guys—when it comes time to settle down, they eventually drift back to their own kind."

I chewed my lip and tried not to think about it. Wick and I were bonding, and no amount of monogramming or madras was going to come between us. And for the next several weeks, nothing did. He was sleeping over most nights, and we were getting along so famously that I even took him to an MTV party.

And then . . . things started to fall apart. Admittedly, we were running out of things to talk about. The pauses during dinner got longer; the texts got shorter. The last night we hung out, we ordered in and watched *300*, his favorite movie (FYI, any man worth dating will love *300*; it means he loves his country, appreciates a strong woman, and has good abs).

The last thing I ever said to Wick—in person, anyway—was a line from the movie as he was leaving my apartment: "Come back with your shield, or on it."

He laughed his deep, throaty, preppy guffaw and trotted down the stairs and out of my life. Sure, I knew we both had a busy few weeks ahead of us—I was moving and he was having minor surgery on his shoulder—but we'd make time; he could dope himself up on Vicodin and lay around while I unpacked boxes.

Or, he could turn into a giant baby and crab and whine incessantly until I flipped out on him.

Wick made his surgery sound like he was having adamantium grafted onto his skeleton, but I don't really have a whole lot of sympathy for men who can't withstand pain. What would King Leonidas say?

But still, I'm surprisingly maternal when it comes to the boys I date. I can't help it; I'm a southern belle at heart. I enjoy having a boyfriend because I like taking care of someone, but I think this works against me; boys don't expect me to be so sweet and often mistake it for obsessive love, especially New York guys. So I've conditioned myself to stay a bitch for as long as possible. But with Wickham, I thought we were past those kinds of games.

I offered several mellow, recuperation-friendly date ideas. He rejected each one, somehow getting grouchier with each response.

"Want me to come over tonight?" I wrote in an e-mail. "I'll make you dinner and rub your ears."

Boys love having their ears rubbed, just like cocker spaniels.

"Shallon," began his terse reply, "I've told you again and again that I have a hole in my shoulder. Maybe this will help you understand why I can't hang out with you right now."

Attached to the e-mail were five graphic, gory pictures of his surgery and incision site.

That was the last straw. As schmoopy and wuvy-dovey as I can be, I can also turn into a shrieking harpy if you offend me.

"*Maybe this will help you understand*?!" I fumed in my reply. "I'm trying to be nice and you respond to me with derision and sarcasm. Don't talk to me again until you can speak to me like a gentleman!"

Harrumph! I forwarded the exchange to all of my friends, who, in typical female yea-sayer fashion, gave me kudos for standing up for myself.

"Good for you, Shall, what a friggin *crybaby*," said Pfeiffer. "My brother had that surgery and played in his basketball game two days later. He's fifteen."

I patted myself on the back and fully expected an apologetic e-mail or text from Wick.

It never came. No call, text, e-mail—nothing. Not ever.

"See," said Klo, convinced she'd been right about our incompatibility all along. "This is what happens when you date by types. He was just too weird and preppy for you. You can't keep changing for the guys you date."

But his Vineyard Vines ribbon belt had nothing to do with it. In fact, he wasn't any different from the emo guys, the actors, the hippies, or the athletes. They were *all* capable of being immature, self-absorbed, and quick to give up. The same animals, just in different clothes. That's how men are built, and we can either fight it or find ways to make it work to our advantage. I was too stubborn to do the latter and so I ended up alone.

The whole affair made me realize that while people think my typecasting is a bad dating strategy, it really has more to do with exploring different sides of my *own* self than finding some archetypal guy. Maybe this was what my mom was trying to teach me all those years ago—that none of us is ever a single "type." Maybe, instead of trying to "change" me, she was just trying to show me that there are a million different facets of my personality, so why stick with just one?

Ideally, I wouldn't rely on my boyfriends to unlock my different dimensions. But if I hadn't been so determined to date a preppy, I never would've given Wick a try. Our relationship let me dust off those preppy parts of myself that I'd buried beneath years of flashy city life. Maybe next I'll date a guy who teaches me to yodel, do taxidermy, or play the stock market. I always hope that I'm just one more boyfriend away from becoming my authentic self. I'm kind of like Scott Bakula in *Quantum Leap*, constantly switching identities, hoping that my next leap will be the leap home.

Ice Cream, You Scream, We All Scream Because If I Deleted You from Facebook You Probably Wouldn't Notice

I've always thought that grocery stores should be organized according to emotion rather than type of food. True, there is often a diet or health food section, but things need to get a little more specific. In my store, there would be a revenge section, full of sharp, pointy, easily spoilable food, or things that are prone to rupturing in your coworker's purse after she "accidentally" forwards your e-mail about snorting Adderall to your supervisor.

There would be a corner full of foods aimed at impressing someone of the opposite sex—strawberries and champagne, items perfect for picnics, and anything conducive to oh-so-subtly showing off your exceptional sexual skills.

And of course, there would be a heartbreak aisle, maybe two. Clearly, I have thought the most about this particular section and its cornerstone food: ice cream. Since the dawn of heartbreak, women have been using ice cream to mend their wounds and drown their sorrows, a sort of triage paste to patch up holes in the heart.

Isn't it time that ice cream makers realize this and start gearing flavors toward their true constituents? Why, in the throes of being dumped, would I want to reach for something called Chubby Hubby? That just seems cruel. How about getting a little bit more specialized? Perhaps . . .

"Cat Lady"
Tastes Like: Four hundred sleeping pills and a bottle of
Popov vodka

"Reruns of *The Golden Girls*"
Tastes Like: Drool and smeared mascara on the body pillow
you've been humping

"He's Probably Just Over on His Minutes, That's All"
Tastes Like: His T-shirt that you refuse to give back and
making your friends text you just to make sure your
phone's working

"His New Girlfriend Has Herpes. I Can Just Tell."
Tastes Like: Valtrex and Wet Seal lip gloss

"Stalking Is Such an Ugly Word"
Tastes Like: A long-lens telescope and the bushes behind
his house

"Googling Robert Pattinson"
Tastes Like: Salty tears, black nail polish, and Hot Topic
snap-on fangs

"Told My Friends I Didn't Call Him but I Lied"
Tastes Like: Wine in a box and an overly rehearsed voice
mail message that conveys "breezy!" not "stuffed to the
gills with Lexapro!"

"In Bed at Ten P.M. on a Friday"
Tastes Like: Three-day-old Chinese food and a purifying
mud mask (this one comes in a commemorative waffle
cone)

"I'm So Alone"
Tastes Like: Mouth-kissing the·dog

Miss Conduct

To the naked eye, my high school years were spent competing in some kind of Suck-up of the Decade competition. I was heavy into student council all four years, did two French exchange programs, and was on winter formal *and* prom court. I wore pastel ribbons in my hair and dressed up for every Spirit Day. But unlike the other kids overly concerned with impressing colleges, I never played a sport. At least not through my school.

I had always tried to avoid playing sports with people my own age. This is not because I enjoy the wisdom and guidance of older athletes, no no. It's because I'm at best a terrible athlete and at worst a serious health hazard to myself and those around me. Take hockey, for example, the sport I enjoy the most, despite my glaring lack of natural ability. The only thing I'm really good at is fighting, drawing penalties, and thinking up clever jeers to holler at the opposing team. The actual "hockey" part of the game? Not really my strong suit.

I had the good sense to realize this early on in my athletic career and wisely avoided playing on my high school's hockey team, which had an actual *Canadian* on it.

So, instead, I skated myself (just barely) over to an extracurricular women's team, the Chicks with Sticks, at the local hockey rink. It took me years to understand why my guy friends sniggered when I told them our team name.

I told people that the Sticks allowed me to play more aggressively and rebelliously than those pansy-ass "conformists" who played for the University High squad.

Yes, I played with *women*, actual grown-ups with husbands and children. They were patient with a newbie like me. At least I thought so at the time.

In hindsight, they were horribly patronizing and smug, but I was fourteen and was used to being talked to that way by adults. I thought it was just a grown-ups thing, like high-waisted jeans or uncoolness.

I played for about six years until college binge-drinking took priority, then pretty much forgot all about hockey until I moved to Manhattan and dated a French-Canadian, an avid player and spectator.

"*John!*" I'd yell in exasperation after one of his tirades on why so-and-so needed to work on his power-play goal percentage. "I don't *care*. No one cares, this is America."

But the truth was, I just wouldn't admit to myself how much I missed playing. Ironically, I might never have picked my stick up again if he hadn't broken up with me. And what a breakup it was!

John was the first guy I dated in the city and he had always been a hateful boyfriend. He was still getting over his ex—with whom he eventually reconciled—and took out all of his angst on me. He once told me, "I would rather see you very, very upset than for me to be inconvenienced in any way."

Yeah, a real prince. But I loved him. He was smart and sexy and could growl like Wolverine as he pressed me up against a wall.

Still, we fought constantly, and I begged him to just let me break it off. I'd hang up on him, delete his number, only to have him suck me back in again with bouquets of flowers and empty promises. He would apologize and blame work stress for our fights, but I never believed him. In his opinion, I wasn't good enough for him, a belief he barely bothered to conceal.

After all, he'd gone to University of Manitoba law school—"It's the Harvard of Canada, Shallon"—and I was just a waitress living in a closet-sized room in SoHo. He couldn't keep the derision out of his voice when he asked me about my writing ambitions, and the masochistic part of me liked it. I already felt like a loser, and having someone verbally confirm it was sickly satisfying.

But still, I tried to make our relationship work. I thought maybe if I became more like him, he'd see that I was in fact his equal. So I adopted a faint yet unmistakable Canadian accent, which, incidentally, I still have.

I've always absorbed accents very easily. My friend Grier says it's because I'm very empathetic. I think it's because I have a shaky core of self-esteem and will gladly shape-shift into someone else to avoid exposing my true personality.

I worked diligently to turn words like "sorry" and "about" into "soary" and "aboat," and added an awkward "eh" to every sentence.

"Why are you doing that?" he'd ask testily through narrowed eyes. "Are you trying to talk like me?"

"Soary, bud, don't know what you're talkin' aboat, eh. Open a can of pop!"

I sounded like I'd had a stroke. But maybe it worked, because five months into our relationship, we finally found some peace.

I decided to take advantage of his good mood. We were out for dinner one night when I told him my mom was coming to visit and that I'd really like him to meet her. He shifted uneasily in his seat but agreed. Feeling cozy and happy, I asked about his recent trip to Montreal for a hockey tournament with twenty of his buddies.

"Oh man, it was awesome!" he laughed. "We all pretended to be the men's Olympic figure-skating team and *everyone* believed it! We ran into this bachelorette party and this one chick totally ate it up. She was pretty ugly though. Jeez, I can't believe I slept with her."

"Wait, *what*?"

He shrugged lamely, not a shred of remorse touching his chiseled face. "Yeah. Oops."

I burst into tears and ran out of the restaurant and into the winter night. I balled up my fists and vowed revenge. He had taken away the one thing I loved most: him. So I wanted to rob him of the only thing he seemed to cherish: hockey. Within a few weeks I had shipped my equipment from a storage locker back home in L.A. out to New York and registered for a team at Chelsea Piers, the same sports complex where he played.

Even after months of dating, he had never invited me to one of his games, despite the fact that he claimed to be one of the best players in Manhattan. He must have figured, correctly, that I would be either bored or so impressed that I'd fall even more in love with him. Neither of which he wanted to deal with.

"Chelsea Piers is where I go to get away from stuff," he'd grumble whenever I'd make the *insane* request to watch him play.

"Stuff like . . . me?"

He would look at me stone-faced for a few seconds, debating just how cruel he should be.

"NoShallonofcoursenot," he'd sigh in one uninterested breath, and head out the door with his hockey bag.

Yes, vengeance would be mine. Chelsea Piers was his home away from home, and I was about to invade. There was just one flaw in my plan: I really sucked at hockey. If I didn't get better, and quick, the only thing I would prove to him was that I was as unsteady on the ice as I was in a relationship.

So I poured all of my money into lessons, trainers, and more lessons. But then something amazing happened: the more I played, the less I cared about running into John. I felt more like my authentic self than I had in years.

Gradually, I did get better. My slapshot improved, and I acquired the ability to hit and cross-check girls with waning remorse.

As I got more and more into the game, I became determined to play for the Brooklyn Blades, an all-women team as vicious and fearsome as their name would suggest. Somehow, I made the team, and our captain strongly encouraged all of us to try out for the Empire State Games. In the grand scheme of competitive hockey, being an ESG champ ranks somewhere just above getting a customer service award from Best Buy, but still, I wanted in.

I signed up for the tryouts, which were being held at a random rink in Harlem, but I was so nervous I made the cab turn around twice. Finally, I called my coach for support, and he shamed me into going ahead with it.

"Look, at the very worst, it's more ice time, right?"

Clearly, he didn't know how ridiculously mean women could be about these things. Well, about lots of things, really. Like how I force my mom to lie about her age because it will in turn make me seem younger.

Sure, my game had improved, but I still didn't feel ready to be on an actual competition team.

First things first, I told myself as I walked into the locker room, *just try to make friends.*

I was flooded with relief when I recognized a girl from my Chelsea Piers league and gradually become comfortable enough to strike up conversations with other girls as we piled on our pads.

And I use the term "girls" loosely. They were built like brick houses. Or bulldogs. Or bulldog-shaped brick houses. Even worse, they had all been playing for at least fourteen years. I have barely been feeding myself for fourteen years.

I would not use the word "awesome" to describe my performance. I seemed to trip on every divot in the ice, and at one point a simple skating drill sent me flying into the boards. Then, while twitchily sipping water to calm my nerves, I spilled it all over the ice and slipped again in the ensuing puddle.

I realized that chatting with all the girls in the locker room had been a terrible mistake. Thanks to me and my big mouth they all knew I played for two different teams, so I couldn't even lie and say this was my first time on the ice. Or maybe that I was recovering from polio and hadn't yet learned to rework my legs. My last resort was to pretend I didn't speak English and wander away, but that was out too.

But as bad as the drills were, it was nothing compared to the total athletic carnage that was the scrimmage. Actual game play is usually my strong suit—I have good "hockey sense" and instincts when it comes to the game, I just can't execute it. And no matter how large my opponent is, I always knock them down. Always. I'm deceptively dense and have very rarely felt guilt of any kind, so I have no problem clotheslining a bitch.

Unfortunately, these other girls were so fast, I just pawed around uselessly as they sidestepped me altogether. I ended up lurching back and forth in front of the goal I was ineptly trying to help defend, much to the ire of the Chevy-sized net-minder, Bianca. As poorly as I was doing, she wasn't faring much better. Easy shots slipped in without her even noticing.

Soon she started wheezing at me to pass here, shoot there, blah blah blah. I hissed over my shoulder for her to be quiet.

"Well I can't *see* with you dancing like a fairy in my line of sight!" she hollered back. "Do you even know what you're supposed to be *doing*?"

I turned around and glared at her, real steely-like. Suddenly all of my old high school fears *and* all of my John-related insecurities leapt back to life. Yes, Bianca, I knew exactly what I should have been doing—but I just couldn't. I should've been brave enough to leave John at the first signs of emotional abuse, but I wasn't. I should have had a job more respectable than waitressing, but I didn't.

In times of crisis, it's suicide or homicide. Fight or flight. I wished desperately that the ice would open up and pull me into a gaping black sea. But the only abyss before me was my own cavernous failure.

So I decided to fight. Not in the Disney-movie sense where I would cowboy up and dazzle everyone on the ice with some unknown reserve of skill and prowess. No, no. I fought using my weapon of choice: hideously inappropriate insults.

"You can't see because you're too damn *fat* to move around the net. I could put a fucking refrigerator in your place and stop more shots!"

Incensed, she stood up on her piggy legs and pulled off her mask.

"A refrigerator?!" she screeched.

"Ohhh, I got your attention now, eh? Too bad I'm not the puck!"

For a split second, I thought she was going to burst into flames with fury. Instead, she whacked her stick on the ice then pointed it at me like a gun.

"Shut your ass up, Lester," she sneered. "You suck at hockey."

The words hit me like a blade to the throat and I gasped. I want more than anything to be good at hockey, but I'm not. The crushing reality hit me: I'm an asthmatic little geek who is better suited to writing a story about sports than actually playing them. I felt tears sting my eyes and mustered up my courage to throw one final arrow her way.

"You know what, honey? At the end of the day, *I'm pretty*. You might win at hockey, but being hot wins at *life!*"

Needless to say, I didn't make the team, nor any friends. I crawled home, utterly defeated, and thought about what a loser I was; I was never going to be better than John at hockey. Not ever.

"You don't have to be," said my friend Christine, scoffing; she had talked me down off all of my John-related cliffs of insanity. "It'd irk him enough just to know you play at all! He thinks he's copyrighted this sport, but all you have to do is inject yourself into it and he'll lose his mind. Can you run into him somehow at the rink? Looking incredibly hot, of course, maybe act like you're dating a professional player?"

I smiled deviously, the wheels of revenge turning in my reptilian little mind.

"Christine," I said slowly, "lies and stalking are things that I can *always* engineer . . ."

Stalktoberfest

In war, truth is the first casualty.
—Aeschylus

When it came to my breakup with John Lombardi, truth was not my friend. I had suffered through the horrible facts of his cheating on me and, in my quest to avenge myself through hockey, had been forced to confront the humiliating reality that I was pretty awful on the ice.

So when I decided to launch a new campaign of emotional terror on John, self-respect was a willing martyr.

Over a year had passed since our split, but Christine's words of advice on how to spite him still rang in my ears.

Oh, Shallon, let it go! I told myself. *You've published a book, gotten a job that doesn't involve non-slip shoes, even learned to skate better—you've already won.*

But revenge isn't about winning; it's about justice. It's about making someone feel just a fraction of the pain and misery he inflicted on you. But still, I tried to be the bigger person, to put our relationship behind me and focus on hockey, the unexpected silver lining. And like I said, the more I played, the less I thought about that hateful retard and all the heartache he caused. But then one day, months after the Empire State Games fiasco, I was at Chelsea Piers for a skating workshop when I saw him—*John*.

I was in the middle of a suicide sprinting drill when I suddenly saw his stocky frame and unmistakable chiseled jaw walking toward the locker room, and I stopped dead in my tracks. Just like Giant Douche had at Houston's, John looked the way I'd remembered him in my happy daydreams—striking and manly. Hidden behind the rink's Plexiglas, a hockey helmet, and a mouth guard, I felt brave enough to stare right at him.

"John . . . ," I murmured hollowly, our six months of turmoil reinfecting my mind like a dormant virus.

Maybe he wasn't all bad, I found myself thinking, already seduced by his Jon Hamm handsomeness. *Maybe it was all my fault.* Just then, John gave a high five to a buddy walking out of the locker room, and as soon as his friend passed, I saw John roll his eyes scornfully. He had that same disdainful sneer that he'd hurled at me so many times. Pff, same old John.

As quickly as it had come, all of those warm, gooey feelings receded and were replaced by that familiar searing hatred, the ugly remnants of our bitter breakup.

I told myself that this was a sign from the gods that the time for comeuppance was nigh.

I rarely plan anything in my life as meticulously as I plan revenge. I've always been a big fan of retribution, mostly because I'm not very good at expressing myself in the moment when I'm actually being screwed over. I know, I know, this seems hard to believe—I'm pretty quick-witted and certainly sassy, but in the face of a breakup, fight with a friend, or reaming by a boss, I just sit there in mute horror. So when I finally *do* decide that no, I do *not* like being cheated on, or no, a 50 percent pay cut is *not* okay with me, the chance to speak up has already passed. I have no choice but to let my vengeance do the talking.

Let me also add that I dole out my revenge responsibly; the recipients of my payback have it coming in a big way. I don't waste my time planning elaborate vendettas against a guy who doesn't call after one bad date or a friend who stained a sweater she borrowed. You have to wound me in a very deep way for my particular brand of hell to arrive at your doorstep.

Over the years, I've gotten much better at revenge. In high school I was obvious and unoriginal in my rage, shoving a girl during PE or telling everyone that Zack Freeman "kissed like a gay guy"—like I even knew what that was supposed to mean.

But once I got to college, I learned that psychological warfare is the most satisfying of all. For example, freshman year there was a guy named Joey who lived a floor below us. He was a leering, drunken brute and would harass and grope all the girls in Trinity Hall. I usually brushed off his foul come-ons and sloppy butt grabs, but when he told my timid suitemate that he'd "pound her in the ass" and made her cry, I'd had enough. I spent the next two weeks learning to pick the lock on my dorm room door, MacGyver style. Why? Because each lock in Trinity Hall was made by the same company, so once you learned to pick one, you could open them all.

Next, I tailed Joey and his roommate Ricky for several days to make sure I had their schedule down. Then, on an afternoon when I knew they were out, I recruited my roommate Lisa to play lookout as I put my nefarious plan into action.

It took me less than six minutes to crack open Joey's dorm room door, wriggle under his bed, deposit "the package," and slip back to my room undetected. "The package" was a mixture of canned tuna, cod liver oil, and an open tin of Fancy Feast. Here I should mention that not only did I go to school in California, but the town was expecting a heat wave, which meant that the putrid mixture would reek like death in no time at all. Plus, because the suite was occupied by eighteen-year-old boys, and disgusting ones at that, finding the stink in that room would be like trying to find an unroofied beer at a Sigma Chi party.

Word of my caper quickly spread among the girls on my floor, and we all waited anxiously for the smelly/glorious horror to begin.

Twenty-four hours later, Lindsay in 4C saw Ricky purchasing three cans of Febreze from Rite-Aid. The day after that, Jen in 2A spotted Joey doing six loads of laundry . . . with extra bleach. By day three, Lisa's sorority sister admitted that she'd tried to hook up with Joey but had to leave because the room smelled so nauseating. After that, things really got bad/awesome: Ricky took to sleeping in the common room and the guys on their floor had signed a petition to kick the two out altogether. Once the campus heard about the two fishy freshmen, their social lives dried up within hours.

At the end of the week, all of us girls watched in smug victory as Joey and Ricky cleared out every piece of garbage from their rancid room and shelled out $200—each!—to have it professionally sanitized.

I never told Joey that I was the one who turned his dorm into a landfill, which is the key to any good plot. Sometimes it can be tempting to take credit for your handiwork (just ask al-Qaeda), but it's a rookie mistake. If you're caught, you just look petty (which you are), plus you run the risk of getting sucked into a tit-for-tat cold war that goes on forever.

But now, all these years later, I'd *have* to reveal my face in order for my plan against John to work. Christine was right; I didn't need to get drafted to the Rangers to get under his skin. I knew my very presence at the rink would be enough to send him into a tizzy.

At first glance, this sounds like child's play—no lock picking or smelly concoction, simply *show up* and watch his blood boil, right? But the devil is in the details. I had to figure out when he'd be at the rink, why, and how I could run into him without making it obvious that I was stalking. Timing would be everything. Even if I *did* get face-to-face with my enemy, what would I say? I'd worry about that later, I told myself. For now, I needed to know his schedule.

It took me nearly a week just to deduce what team he was on. I spent hours combing through the Chelsea Piers team rosters online, but I couldn't find his name anywhere. Finally, I resorted to calling the rink and pretending that I'd found a shin guard with his name on it.

"I could drop by before his game," I said in a fake southern accent (it just seemed necessary). "What team is he on, darlin'?"

The teenage employee revealed that John was a sub on the Ice Hogs, part of the elite league. Aha! A sub! *Loser.* That would also explain why I hadn't seen his name on the roster . . . but now he'd be even harder to track since he wasn't a regular player.

So I turned to math. Sifting through the Ice Hog stats sheet, I deduced that John played about 60 percent of their games—not the best odds, but it was all I had. Their championship playoff game was next Wednesday at seven P.M. and I knew John wouldn't miss it. Even if he wasn't playing, he'd be there. I circled the date on my calendar and told my roommates to be home for dinner—Operation Stalktoberfest was about to commence and I needed their help.

"Eeeee, yay!" Marcia squealed as I laid out the plan. "I love a good stalk!"

I presented a large, hand-drawn map of the Chelsea Piers Sky Rink and parking structure, with the two possible entrances marked with big red Xs. I'd need an accomplice stationed at each one, because John could take either depending on whether he arrived via cab or subway.

"I'm going to hang this map here in the kitchen so we can all get familiar with it before Stalktoberfest," I said authoritatively. "This will be your basic hammer-and-anvil assault, but if you guys prefer we can do a flanking maneuver and close the net on—"

"I'm sorry," Pfeiffer said, interrupting. "What are you talking about? Hammers?"

"It's a tactical maneuver, *duh*." I sighed. "Basically you two flush him toward me and then I crush him, in conjunction with a circumvallation. *Obviously.*"

The girls just stared at me.

"I feel like you just started speaking in tongues," said Marcia.

Thanks to two years in army ROTC during college, I'd learned all sorts of tactical maneuvers, which helped me step up my revenge game considerably. Preliminary bombardment, creeping barrages, decentralized command—I knew them all. And as such, I had become one badass mothafucka to mess with.

Once I'd translated my plan into language Pfeiff and Marcia could understand, I needed to make doubly sure my logistics were sound. I spent one solid afternoon prowling around Chelsea Piers, interrogating security guards and employees about other exits and entrances I might not have considered.

"What about those stairs?" I asked Jose, the parking attendant. "Could someone access the Sky Rink from those?"

"Oh no," he said in a thick Spanish accent. "Those are jus' for emergency, *mija*."

Once I felt satisfied that my perimeter was solid, I took snaps on my cell phone and forwarded them to the girls, along with their "scripts."

Since we didn't know where John would enter the complex, they both had to be prepared to "groom the dog," as I dubbed it. This meant that when John approached, whichever one of them was closer would pretend to be on her cell phone and say loudly, within earshot of John: "Wanna go to the Oilers game tonight? . . . Yeah, one of the players has a crush on Shallie and sent them to her office!"

John loved the Oilers and his ears would surely perk at the mention of his favorite NHL team. This would ensure that he would hear my nickname but would be so distracted at the mention of his precious team he would forget all about it . . . until of course he encountered me upstairs. Then the overheard conversation would suddenly resurface.

A player has a crush on Shallie? My Shallie?! he would think hysterically, and wonder just how deeply I had infiltrated his beloved hockey world. During our relationship, John made it very clear that I was never to encroach on *his* sport, even though I'd played for years. The game was *his*, and if I ever suggested that I come see him play he made me feel like a mistress threatening to call his wife. And yet there I'd be, invading his precious world of pucks and pads with a team of my own.

I tingled with fiendish delight just thinking about it.

Once the fake phone call took place, they were to use walkie-talkies to tell me, "The dog is approaching the kennel."

"Why don't I just call you on your phone?" Marcia asked.

"Because I already bought walkie-talkies."

"But . . . isn't that going to be kind of odd?" she asked, pressing me. "You sitting in the bleachers with a *walkie-talkie* crackling?"

Of course she was right, but I told her that it was too late to deviate now and pulled out two black wigs from my purse.

"That'd better be a puppy," Pfeiffer said as I plopped the hairpieces on the table.

"You guys are going to need disguises."

"Shallon, he's never met us," Marcia said. "And even if he *did* recognize us, we're mentioning you by name, so . . ."

"And I already *have* black hair," said Pfeiff, "so I'm not sure how much good this 'disguise' will do."

I sighed and wondered if Eisenhower had this much trouble planning D-Day. I finally coaxed Marcia into the wig and sent the girls to bed. In twenty-four hours Operation Stalktoberfest would commence, and we all needed our rest. Being creepy takes a lot of energy.

The next day, I spent an hour getting ready: perfectly wavy hair, subtle-yet-sexy makeup, a low-cut tank top, and yoga pants.

"So, what are you going to say to him exactly?" asked Marcia as the three of us headed out the door.

"Um . . ."

I had no idea. I recalled the Joker's line in *The Dark Knight*: "I'm like a dog chasing a car—what would I do if I actually caught it?"

I would act cool and serene, a far cry from the pathetic, broken girl he'd left all those months ago. I figured that we would chat amiably for a few minutes; I'd look irresistible, oh-so-casually mention that I too played at Chelsea Piers, then watch him slink miserably away.

What actually happened was both infinitely better and infinitely worse.

It started off smoothly enough. The girls got into position as I took my post in the bleachers of the east rink, where I would pretend to watch my (nonexistent) friend play in the Sled Dogs game.

At approximately 18:35 the target made contact with our envoy at entrance point Bravo; Pfeiffer ran through the fake phone call perfectly as Marcia radioed that he was en route.

My stomach did a somersault as he walked through the door. He was so beautiful in his haughtiness, so untouchably lovely, like a marble bust. My icy heart instantly softened.

I called out his name and broke into a smile . . . and he practically broke into a run.

"What are *you doing here?*" He scowled, jerking his neck back. You'd think he'd run into Hitler.

Well hello to you too, Buttercup. "I'm watching my friend's game," I laughed, just *soooo* shocked at the coincidence. I put my arms around him and felt him stiffen.

Now, okay, I should probably come clean on something. There was more to our breakup than just his cheating on me: after we split, I was so hurt and angry that I wrote about his infidelities on my blog for the entire world to read. You'd think that I would've learned my lesson after the Giant Douche debacle just a few weeks prior, but no.

Since John had never listened to a word I said when we were dating, I never imagined he'd *deliberately* look to read my website. But he had. And "upset" does not do his reaction justice. John had been *furious* and sent a scathing e-mail telling me I was vicious, hateful, and deserved a lifetime of pain.

I had felt slightly guilty at airing our dirty laundry on the web but reminded myself that *he* cheated on *me*; a few snarky blog posts wasn't an eye for an eye—it was an *eyelash* for an eye. Plus, that was all in the past; I thought that the statute of limitations on my comparatively minor offense had run out by now. I was wrong. I'd hoped we were a misdemeanor, but I guess we were a felony.

"Aww, do you still hate me too much to hug me?" I said playfully, trying to hide my trembling hands.

"No, a hug was given," he said, sounding like an IRS agent confirming the status of my tax return.

A hug was given. Wow. *Really?* It was going to be like that after nearly *two years?* We managed to chat for a few minutes before he inched away from me like a nervous dog. However, in between a few inanities about our jobs and new apartments, I managed to work in the fact that I played hockey at Chelsea Piers now too.

"Wait . . . ," he said, looking like someone had punched him in the throat. "You play? *Hockey.*"

"Yes, I play," I said. "Actually, in a way, it's thanks to you. If you hadn't gone on and on about the game I never would've realized how much I missed it!"

He gasped, disgusted. This had been my plan all along, of course, but it was a Pyrrhic victory. I had proved I still had the power to get under his skin, but for what? I didn't want John to hate me. I wanted him to *love* me—then *and* now. Part of me thought he'd see me perched cutely in the bleachers and remember all of our good times: our mornings at the Comfort Diner eating French toast, the kisses while he shaved, the afternoon delight on his lunch break. But he didn't. What leapt into his mind was Shallon the Burdensome, Shallon the Petty, and this little encounter, I realized, would do little to make him think otherwise.

A German proverb says that a great war leaves the country with three armies: an army of cripples, an army of mourners, and an army of thieves. That day, I was serving in them all.

Penns and Needles

Navigating New York with a broken bone is a huge pain in the ass. It's also a great way to get laid.

I've always been much better at handling physical pain than mental anguish. When I was twenty-three, the guy at the dry cleaner told me I looked old, so I cried for two days and scheduled an appointment for Botox. But when I was eight and compound-fractured my arm roller skating, I actually fell asleep on the car ride to the doctor. It's a good thing that I'm so cool in such a crisis, because I'm very clumsy.

After my cracked arm, my next big injury was in seventh grade, when I was thrown off a horse. Let me tell you, you've never known pain until you've tried to pull a cowboy boot off a broken ankle. I spent three god-awful months on crutches and have a permanent hoof-shaped bruise on the inside of my foot. But still, I considered it a cakewalk compared to the dry cleaner incident.

Six years later, my best friend, Ellen, and I were at a water park when my face hit the back of her head going down a slide, smashing my nose to bits.

But at least back then I had a mama to help me bathe, make me snacks, and do my laundry while I convalesced. If you have to be injured someplace, Irvine, California, is a pretty ideal location, especially when you have a professional nurse for a parent.

Needless to say, my mother wasn't thrilled when I moved to New York—a city full of open manholes and pokey objects—*and* resumed playing hockey.

I pointed out that in all my years on the ice, I'd never been seriously injured.

"Oh really?" she retorted. "Are you forgetting the three concussions you had in high school?"

Actually yes, I had forgotten them; that's how head injuries work. But I didn't even mind concussions. They were kind of fun. I turned into a babbling idiot and said all sorts of nonsense, much to the delight of my friends. For a few hours, I was the life of the party . . . until I started throwing up and foaming at the mouth.

I promised her I'd be careful and for three years, I was. Until that fateful St. Patrick's Day in 2007 when I broke my elbow. I slipped on an icy patch of sidewalk—sober!—and threw my arms out behind me to break my fall. At first I thought maybe I'd just thrown my back out of alignment—nothing that a few more beers couldn't anesthetize. But as my friends and I ambled into the next bar, I realized I couldn't straighten out my left arm.

"You guys, I think this is bad," I said as they lined up whiskey shots. "I can't move my arm."

They scoffed. "Eh, I'm sure it's okay. It's a good thing you're a righty!"

"I'm left-handed."

"Whatever," Marcia said, handing me a shot. "Tomayto, tomahto! Here, pound this."

I took the drink with my right hand and flung half of it down my shirt. Covered in Jameson, I decided to call it a night. I hoped that some aspirin and ice would fix whatever was wrong; the idea of going to the ER the day after St. Patty's was unappealing, to say the least. But after I woke up with my left arm seized up against my chest like a chicken wing, it was time to let a medical professional take a look.

I draped a coat awkwardly around my shoulders as best I could with one hand and hopped a cab to St. Vincent's.

The ER was surprisingly quiet and empty, save for a few drunken homeless men and the large black women working the intake desk, who were delighted to admit someone sane.

"Oh, honeychild, wussa matter, now? You hurt yo'self?" one of them asked.

"Yeah," I squeaked, knee-deep in self-pity. "I think I broke my arm."

"Well you just sit on down here and we gon' have us a look," she said reassuringly, rubbing my back with her massive hand as she led me to an empty bed.

"The docta gon' be right on in, now. Don't you worry your little head about a thang. Just fill out these forms best ya can wit yo' good arm."

I fumbled with the clipboard full of papers and suddenly missed my mama very much. Since she was the nurse in the family, I relied on her to do things like this while I was busy feeling sorry for myself and complaining about the magazine selection. During every one of my medical maladies, she had pulled the physician aside and explained in a low tone that she was an RN and that he could speak plainly to her and ignore me altogether. She'd then translate the prognosis to me in one of three ways:

1. **"Garbo could handle it."** Translation: no big deal. Garbo was our beloved cocker spaniel and was constantly finding herself in some sort of calamity, whether it was vomiting up rat poison or being stung by wasps or getting horrible ear infections. But no matter how sick she was, she'd take a nap on the cool tile of the foyer and wake up feeling fine.

2. **"We should probably stop at Blockbuster."** This meant there would be some downtime, but my biggest enemy would be boredom, so multiple videos would be needed. If I was going to be uncomfortable, she'd let me rent my favorite Liza Minelli movie, *Steppin' Out*, but I knew I didn't *really* need to panic until she said . . .

3. **"I think I'll make some butterscotch pudding!"** She made pudding only when I was having surgery. Once upon a time I probably liked butterscotch pudding, but over the years I developed a Pavlovian response to the dessert—pudding equaled misery.

I had just eased myself onto the tissue-paper-covered table when an X-ray tech arrived, and ten minutes later I was flopped on the crunchy exam table like a pound of pastrami.

My arm was throbbing and every bone in my back felt out of place, like a Lego castle put together wrong. Finally, the doctor arrived. She was young and pretty-ish, and, best of all, blond. I feel more comfortable around flaxen people. Brunettes are full of nasty surprises—unibrows, upper-lip hair, unintelligible accents—but blondes are lovely and always smell like Sun-Ripened Raspberry body spray. It's in our DNA.

"Well," the pretty doctor said with a sigh, "looks like your elbow is broken."

"Okay . . . what does this mean?" I said slowly.

"It means you fractured a bone in your elbow."

"So like . . . videos? Or pudding, do you think?"

She squinted, obviously disappointed that a patient whom she assumed would be lucid was in fact not.

"Sling, actually," she said, pulling one out of the cupboard. "We don't put broken elbows in casts. Wear this for about six weeks and then do physical therapy."

I groaned; I *hated* physical therapy. It went on forever and was equal parts boring and painful.

On the way out, she handed me a massive pill.

"Here's a Percocet; it should help with the pain. And I'm giving you a prescription for a thirty day supply."

"A painkiller?" I said, puzzled. As the daughter of a medical professional, you might think I enjoyed a smorgasbord of lovely drugs, but oh no. Whether I'd had surgery or a stubbed toe, I'd never ingested anything stronger than ibuprofen; my family believed in working through the pain—any pain—*au naturel*. One time at a family brunch with all my aunts and cousins, the older women started telling childbirth stories. I mentioned something about the miracle of epidurals and the entire table laughed.

"Yeah, right," my mom said between guffaws, "you're not getting an epidural, honey."

My ninety-eight-year-old aunt Sally nodded in agreement. "That's not our way."

Margaret, my great-grandmother and de facto nanny, had a home remedy for almost every ailment. She whipped up mystery salves and balms for everything from chest colds to splinters and during the Great Depression used to employ maggots to cleanse wounds and "draw out the poison." To her, things like anesthesia and morphine were hilariously newfangled. Still, somehow, her curious concoctions always seemed to work.

But that was then and this was now, and my arm felt like it was on fire, so I swallowed the pill gratefully and left the hospital with my arm in a sling. Fifteen minutes later, I started hallucinating. Decaf coffee is too strong for me, so I don't know why I thought that a giant Percocet was going to sit well. My stomach lurched and my field of vision split in two as the cab swooped around the corner to my block. I tumbled out of the car and somehow managed to crawl up three flights of stairs to my apartment, clinging to the banister for dear life. Sweating and shaking, I burst through the door and collapsed on the ground.

My roommates helped me into bed, and even through my doped-up haze, I was furious. All I had wanted was a respite from pain, not a magical mystery tour.

I slept for eighteen hours until the meds wore off and the dull throb in my elbow woke me up. Clearheaded, I decided not to let this injury get me down. We shall overcome! That buoyant feeling lasted exactly ten more minutes until it dawned on me that with only one working hand—my *non-dominant* hand—I was basically helpless. Everything from making food to putting on my coat became nearly impossible. Doing my hair was out of the question, so for the next six weeks I was at the mercy of the humidity index. Although it didn't much matter that I looked like an extra in a Whitesnake video; I couldn't really go out and risk getting jostled in a crowd anyway. Plus, I couldn't figure out how to fasten my bra.

That's fine, I told myself, *I'll just throw myself into work!* But since I couldn't type, I just sat around the *FHM* offices reading old issues and bothering everyone. Eventually my bosses told me to stay home until I was well enough to write again.

So I sat on the couch and did the only thing I still could: (slowly and laboriously) text my newest flame. For the past few months, I'd been in a hot-and-heavy text-based relationship with a professional tennis player whom I called Penn, like the tennis ball. We had met through my editor at *FHM*, who had casually mentioned during an interview that there was a female editor (me) who had a crush on him.

"Really?" Penn had said incredulously, "On *me*? Here, give her my number."

People think that celebrities are hard to date, but they're not. You just have to meet them in the right context.

Once we started talking—sorry, *texting*—it was on. We spent four hours a day with our fingers glued to our phones. I felt like I'd known him my whole life, which, *I know*, is exactly what people say about the psycho they meet on a World of Warcraft message board who eventually kills them. But my love for him was good and pure. And it wasn't the fame that did it, either. I had dated celebrities before and they were fun to bat around, like shiny balls of foil. But I actually *respected* Penn.

Growing up, my life was devoid of men. No father, grandpa, uncle, brother—even my pets were female. Men were always foreign and strange to me, and most whom I had known in adulthood had proved themselves to be weak creatures ruled by their fragile egos who would cut and run when the going got tough. Penn was different.

When he was thirteen, he sank his teeth into the dream of being a professional athlete, and he never looked back. Prom nights, study abroad, spring break, twenty-first-birthday benders—he sacrificed all of them as he chased his tennis dream. But like I said, successful men were nothing new to me. Only unlike the various douche bankers and solipsistic musicians I generally ended up dating, Penn neither complained nor crowed. And there was just something innocent about him; he had a wide-eyed sense of wonder about the most ordinary things—Jet Skis, skyscrapers, dirty martinis. Outwardly, he seemed to be taking life by the horns, but in reality he'd experienced very little of it off the tennis court.

"I think you're getting a little carried away with this," my friends said. "You guys haven't even met!"

They made a valid point. He lived and trained in Pennsylvania (another reason I called him Penn) and I was starting to wonder if we would ever lay eyes on each other. But it didn't matter. While most people in my position would have gotten hooked on the generous supply of Percocet I'd been given, Penn was my drug of choice. We texted so much that I finally got a cramp in my right hand and couldn't move it for over an hour, prompting a screaming, crying fit; I needed to write him back! He would be worried!

Hysterical, I called my roommate Pfeiffer—*with my toe*—and demanded that she return from the gym and text Penn for me.

"Okay, this has gone far enough," she huffed on the other end of the phone. "I'm coming home, all right, and getting your crazy ass in the shower. We're going out for Holly's birthday tonight."

The second I walked into the restaurant, I realized instantly that cloistering myself away for all that time had been a huge mistake.

Every man in the place was staring at me. At first I assumed they were gawking at my erratic eyeliner or off-center hair clip. But then I recognized the look in their eyes. I'd seen it before, on Animal Planet, when a lion spotted a weak, limping wildebeest dawdling behind the rest of the pack. I was the dating equivalent of that wildebeest: easy prey.

"Here, let me get that for you," said a handsome man in a suit, appearing out of nowhere and peeling off my coat.

"Allow me, miss," said another guy as he pulled out my chair.

My friends stared, openmouthed, in disbelief and envy. The manager stopped by our table to wish Holly a happy birthday, but as soon as he spotted my sling, he scuttled over and knelt down by my chair.

His name was Declan, an impishly cute Irish fellow with a mischievous Robert Pattinson smile. He was witty and charismatic, but then again I'd spent a fortnight in the company of *Law & Order* reruns—a traffic cone would've piqued my attention. He ended up comping half our meal—an "injury rebate," he called it—and asking me out for the following weekend.

My roommates were overjoyed. Not only would they get a night in the apartment without me ambling around like Boo Radley, but maybe I'd fall for Declan and shut the hell up about Penn for a little while.

I had to admit that I was excited to spend my evening with something other than the new-message chime, and Declan had made reservations at the Little Owl, a charming place in the West Village.

I considered forgoing the sling, but the girls reminded me that it was the reason he'd fallen for me in the first place (certainly not my personality), so I strapped it back on.

Declan looked dashing in a crisp suit and pink tie, and for the first half hour of our date, things went swimmingly. He was just as clever and rakish as he was the night we met . . . and then I said six little words that would alter the course of our date completely.

"Tell me a secret about yourself."

This is my go-to first-date question. It fosters a sense of bonding and intimacy, and how much a person is willing to share reveals a lot about them. In Declan's case, it revealed way too much. This is the story he told me:

"So all through high school I was really into theater [author's note: RED FLAG] and my best friend was a total jock—captain of the football team, all that. One summer we were out at my parents' lake house and he was like, 'Dude . . . I think I'm gay.' And I was like, 'Really? Well, how are you going to find out for sure?' And . . . well, Shallon . . . that was the first time I had a cock in my mouth."

It isn't very often that I'm rendered speechless. But I stared at Dec in mute, wide-eyed horror like he'd bitten the head off a rabbit. I didn't even blink. The *first* time he'd had a wiener in his mouth.

Keep in mind, this was only our second conversation ever. If he considered this a level-one, "my middle name is Francis" type of secret, I could only imagine what monstrosities awaited me down the road in our relationship. And I didn't want to know.

I trudged home after a hasty meal and broke the news to my roommates that Declan was not exactly straight as an arrow. Still, despite his rainbow-colored past, the girls were optimistic that we could make things work, especially if it meant letting go of my Penn obsession.

"So let me get this right," I said testily, "you'd rather have me date a *gay guy*—"

"Gay-*ish*, Shallon," Marcia said, correcting me. "Not totally gay, just gay-*ish*!"

I rolled my eyes. "Fine, a gay-*ish* guy in person rather than have a text-message relationship with a hetero professional athlete?"

"Yes," they said in unison. "Yes we would."

Of course they would. The prospective tales I'd bring home after dates with Declan—trysts with barnyard animals, amateur porn, amputee-fetish conventions—would be far more interesting than yet another rundown of banal SMSs about ground strokes and forehand volleys.

I decided to compromise and give Declan one last shot. We met up for lunch and as soon as I saw him, the Ick settled over me like a lead blanket. He was wearing jeans—*rolled up*. One look at his scrawny, pale ankles and all I could picture was him leaping around the set of *Mamma Mia!* playing grab-ass with his boyfriend Sergio.

I cut off the relationship then and there, saying that my elbow was too much of a distraction. The argument made no sense, clearly, but neither did Declan's admission of wiener play. Sometimes you have to fight stupid with stupid.

Much to Pfeiffer and Marcia's ire, I burrowed back into my phone, ensconced in the warm safety of Penn. Aside from the fact that we'd never met each other, our relationship was, in a way, perfect. All I really need from a boyfriend is constant attention—it doesn't have to be in person. Penn's relentless texting was the perfect amount of distraction and titillation. Our imaginations filled in the gaps in the relationship—gaps like actual physical contact. Rightly or wrongly, I couldn't shake my addiction to him—the incessant stream of communication, the proud thrill of seeing him on TV, hearing an arena full of people chant his name. They were all things that I wanted for myself, and I was living, in a way, through him. He was a contact high, and I was perfectly willing to chase him around forever, hoping for one more whiff of his intoxicating scent.

"I wouldn't put your eggs in this basket," Holly said one afternoon. "He's probably texting a ton of other girls too."

Possible, but unlikely—he simply didn't have the time. I knew where he was every minute of the day. I knew when his plane took off after a match and when it landed back in Pittsburgh. Once, he even texted me *during* an ESPN interview on TV: "*This guy is such a retard.*"

I responded with something pithy and delightedly watched Penn giggle at his phone and wink at the camera.

One night, Pfeiffer and Marcia came marching into my room and issued a proclamation: I had one month to meet Penn in person (no Skyping allowed) or they were signing me up for eHarmony.

Reluctantly, I agreed. They were right; something had to give. So I passed along the ultimatum and held my breath as I waited for him to respond. Twenty agonizing minutes ticked by and still no reply. Was he laughing? Deleting my number? Furious that I'd make such an outlandish demand like meeting face-to-face?

I started to shake and sweat, panic and regret spreading through my chest. *This is it*, I thought, *I'm never going to hear from him again. I've blown it.*

Just then, my phone chimed.

"*I have a tourney in Jersey three weeks from now. You have 3 tickets at will call under your name. I'll kiss that broken elbow and make it better! :)*"

My heart leapt! I held the text up for my friends to *oooh* and *ahh* at, like it was a newborn Simba in *The Lion King*.

I spent the next few weeks obsessing over what I was going to wear, even changing my mind one last time on the car ride over. I was so anxious that I nearly threw up.

After I sat nervously through the match (he won), we waited in the stands for Penn to shower and change as the crowd filed out.

I'll never forget the sight of him walking out of the arena tunnel and into my life. The intense angles of his muscular frame were softened by a perfectly tailored black suit, while his dark, wavy hair glistened in the cooling twilight.

"Hey." He grinned softly, but that simple word, those three wee letters, spoke volumes to my heart.

H. *Here comes the bride. Honey, start the car, the baby's coming!*

E. *Eternity. Ever after.*

Y. *Yell it from the rooftops. You complete me.*

"Hi," I murmured back as he pulled me close for a lingering kiss on the cheek. He smelled clean and fresh, like an afternoon nap on newly laundered sheets. I buried my nose in his neck as Pfeiffer bit back a giggle.

"I thought you were going to take a bite out of him!" she said later, laughing.

I would've swallowed him whole if I could have, like a snake, and walked around proudly with a Penn-shaped bulge in my gut. Instead we just smiled at each other goofily.

"Did you guys have fun?" His voice was barely above a whisper, but it didn't matter. Our eyes were talking enough for the both of us, drinking each other in—the silent, unerring language of eye contact.

A few minutes of small talk passed in a dreamlike blur until his coach came out and hollered for him to get on the bus. He drew me close for a farewell hug and whispered in my ear, "Come to my hotel tonight—the Affinia Dumont, eleven o'clock. I have a surprise . . ."

And with that he was gone, my heart lurching and my mind swimming at the idea of seeing him again . . . at night . . . *alone.*

"Well, I guess that's that!" said Marcia brightly on the car ride home. "I have this *gorgeous* trader that I want to set you up with. He's from Westchester and—"

"Wait, what? What do you mean, 'that's that'?"

She and Pfeiffer exchanged exasperated glances.

"*I mean*," she said slowly, "that now you've met him and the spell is broken; you got what you wanted, right?"

I considered my answer carefully. In no way was that five-minute encounter enough to slake my thirst for him. But I wasn't willing to admit that to my friends. After all, what kind of addict goes around telling her friends when she's about to score her next fix? Penn was the most private and valuable thing I'd ever had. We existed inside the narrow windows of our cell phones, flourishing in each other's humid imaginations. No one else would understand.

So I lied and told Marcia that yes, I had sweated out the Penn fever and was back to my old self, and to prove it, I was going to meet Declan that very night for drinks.

Unfortunately, I'm a terrible liar and Pfeiffer and Marcia confronted me in my doorway as I left.

"This," Pfeiffer said sternly, "has *got to stop.*"

I tried to evade them, but they weren't having any of it. "I don't know what you're—"

"We know where you're going and, Shallon, you gotta let this thing go. You don't know him—you know a version of him, an idea. Is this *really* all you want out of a relationship? Clandestine meetings at his hotel and text overage charges?"

I winced; she was right. I knew that this lovesick mania had to end sooner or later. It was consuming me, preventing me from meeting an actual, real guy. That night would be my last drink of him, then I'd go cold turkey.

But he's the kind of boy you deserve, whispered my weak, romance-addled brain. *He's tall and handsome and successful!* True, but this wasn't the kind of *relationship* I deserved.

In the cab to his hotel, I steeled my will against his charms and tried to summon the Ick.

"Hey," he said with the same boyish, sleepy smile from the afternoon, looking gorgeous in pajama pants and a tatty T-shirt. He grabbed my wrist and pulled me in for the most perfect kiss in the history of kisses. I'm pretty sure my knees buckled, and I felt any will to hate him turn to dust and blow away. Still woozy from the kiss, I let Penn lead me to the couch, where I was surprised to see a contraption that looked like a cross between a water cooler and a douche. I shot him a puzzled look.

"It's a Cryo Cuff!" he said proudly.

"A what?"

"I figured it'll make your elbow feel a lot better so I had my trainer bring it up."

He swung the contraption around to face me, and with the flick of a switch, it came whirring to life. Penn strapped a blood-pressure-type cuff around my elbow. Icy cold water flowed through the tube into the cuff and within seconds it was like a cool, firm hand pressed around my broken joint, squeezing the inflamed tendons into submission.

It had been years since a boy had been so thoughtful to me. I kicked myself, trying again to hate him. I focused in on how pigeon toed he was and the fact that he used odd, after-school-special-type phrases like "squash the beef." That night, as he slept, I studied his face, desperately searching for a grotesque flaw. But there were none anywhere, on the inside or outside.

After that night, he and I still talked, but not as frequently; I forced myself to pull back and we weaned ourselves gradually. Within a few weeks I met Lord Voldemort, whom I came to love more broadly than Penn, but somehow much less. Voldy understood me, but Penn had *inspired* me. He was everything I wanted to be: humble, driven, focused, and sweet. But I knew in my heart that despite it all, he hadn't been the one for me.

Sometimes I still instinctively reach for my phone to text him, like the alcoholic who forgets, just for a moment, that she's recovered and absentmindedly grabs her dinner companion's drink.

But I put it down and try in vain to get that same dizzying thrill from more rational things like low-cal Frappuccinos and boys from Massachusetts named Charles. A life of sanity and dignity, I know, takes time.

A Pain in the Duff

I don't have a very unique look. I realize this. I'm fair and blond and green eyed, average height and average weight. Physically, I don't stand out very much, unless of course you're Hitler, in which case I'm what you see when you daydream. When I was four years old, I stood in front of the mirror and took stock of my face.

Well, Shallon, I thought, *you're rather plain. Pleasing, but plain. If you want to get noticed it's going to be on personality, not looks. Now, where are your animal crackers?*

I was on the right track with this whole personality thing. Thanks to my inherent weirdness and endless string of dating debacles, I eventually landed myself an MTV reality TV show, *Downtown Girls.* That's when I decided that not all attention is good attention. My reality TV peers don't always agree with this. They'll release sex tapes willy-nilly or tweet that they have a UTI. But we Downtown Girls tried to keep it classy; we peed with the door shut and always wore underwear on blustery days.

But as filming got under way, I learned the hard way that no matter how well-behaved you are, not every stranger on the street is happy that you are making a reality show and won't hesitate to tell you. But things started to turn around once it dawned on me to capitalize on my un-unique physical appearance. If I wanted people to stop freaking out every time an MTV cameraman happened to catch them in a shot, I had to do only one thing: convince them I was Hilary Duff.

For years people had been telling me I looked like the Disney star and I always rolled my eyes. This was out of sheer jealousy, of course. She was younger, more famous than me, *and* married to a Canadian hockey player, which is basically all I want out of life. Secretly, I love her music and I watch *Raise Your Voice* at least once a month, but I'm too bitter to ever admit it openly. She's living out *my* dreams and I simply won't publicly condone that sort of identity theft. So imagine my delight when I got the chance to hijack *her* life.

It was the third week of filming and for the people in our Tribeca neighborhood, the novelty of seeing a reality show in the making had officially worn off.

"Hey, sluts!" someone shouted from the sidewalk. "Yeah, I'm talkin' to you, ya blond Barbie cunt. You're a fuckin' nobody; get the hell off our street!"

"This is *my* street too, ugly!" I spat back. "I live a block away!"

"Get the *fuck out of here!*" screamed one disgruntled (and clearly not yet caffeinated) patron of our local coffee shop simply because our fifteen-person crew stormed the café to film a scene.

I could've pulled out a PowerPoint presentation on why I deserved to be getting my iced tea in that particular coffeehouse, but it wouldn't have mattered. All people needed to see were a boom mic and a camera and they hated me automatically. If I had been an actual celebrity, this would not have been the case. If it were Julia

Roberts or . . . hmm, who are the kids talking about these days . . . Maury Povich filming a show, gasps of awed delight would have echoed through the corridors of Tribeca. But once our good neighbors figured out that my friends and I had never won an Oscar or tested some deadbeat's paternity, we were about as welcome as a case of bedbugs. Soon it started to feel normal for a woman to ram me with her stroller and another guy to let his dog urinate all over our microphone pack.

"Whatever, they're just jealous," Klo sniffed. "That's a good thing. It means we're winning at life."

I like to be envied as much as the next girl, but I'm more of the opinion that a little jealousy goes a long way. Too much smells like dog pee, and I wasn't about to stand for it.

That night we headed out to Cake Shop, a dive bakery on the Lower East Side that doubles as an indie music joint at night.

"What should we wear?" asked Nikki, our resident fashionista. "This place sounds grungy."

The last time I went to Cake Shop I was drunk out of my mind and ended up going home with the heroin-addicted lead singer of an emo band. But I politely chose to withhold the fact that this was the general vibe of the Cake Shop crowd and told the girls to dress pretty.

Literally anything would've been better than the pink sequined dress I chose to wear—a turban, an SS uniform, a skort—anything. The second we walked in, people started booing.

"Look!" sneered one grungy girl in a tatty Black Flag tee, "it's hipster Barbie! Where's your Ken doll, you stupid bitch?"

The mangy crowd roared and toasted her with their PBRs. I turned crimson and her snaggle-toothed friend, smelling weakness, decided to get in a few potshots too.

"Yeah, fucking Paris Hilton bitch! Go make a sex tape, ho!"

"She's Hilary Duff, not Paris Hilton!" Klo hollered back as a joke, but suddenly, the hipsters went silent. The punks and rockabillies craned their tattooed necks to get a better look as Hilary's name rippled through the crowd.

"Oh my God, I think they believed me," Klo murmured as we inched cautiously toward the bar and ordered drinks.

"So . . . I," said the guy waiting for his Maker's Mark, raising his pierced eyebrow at me, "you're Hilary Duff, huh?"

I pursed my lips in a Duffian way and giggled coyly. "You tell me . . ."

"I'm not gonna lie," he said, "my little sister loves you. *And* your ex in that band—what's his name?"

"Joel Madden," I cooed, letting my hair fall in front of my face as camouflage. "He's actually on his way here, but don't make a fuss."

"Omigod," the guy said, not even bothering to conceal his excitement. "Here? He's coming here?! Wow! Wait, I thought you guys broke up?"

"We did . . . but what Mike doesn't know won't hurt him."

I winked and slid away. Lying to drunk boys is my specialty; it helps to keep my mind sharp, kind of like Sudoku does for regular people. But lying about a celebrity's life is a slippery slope; it's a lot easier to get caught pretending to be Hilary Duff than the heir to, say, the Ziploc fortune. But if it kept people from throwing rocks at us, it was a risk I was willing to take.

"You're much prettier in person," a girl said randomly to me in line for the bathroom. It occurred to me that when people talk to celebrities, they seem to start in the middle of the conversation, with an out of nowhere non sequitur sentence. "And you're taller too!"

"Oh, yeah." I blushed. This was starting to get awkward. I love awkward. "It's not that I'm short, it's that everyone in Hollywood is really tall."

"They are?" she said, baffled. "I thought Tom Cruise was practically a midget."

"No," I said, "he's over six feet, swear to snaps!"

"Really!"

"Yep, same with Ryan Seacrest. They're both gigantic."

Mercifully, our producer yanked us out of there before I could embarrass myself/Hilary any further.

I was forced to emulate the Duffster a few more times during filming, but only in emergencies, like the time at the Jersey shore when a girl shoved me against a pinball machine and threatened to cut my hair.

"Hey!" Nikki yelled. "Nobody messes with Hilary Duff's hair—nobody!"

"Oh. Oh, um, gosh I'm sorry, we just . . . we didn't recognize her. Sorry."

Once filming wrapped I decided to retire my Hilary impersonation for good; I could hardly become a legitimate celebrity if I was constantly pretending to be a different one.

But the road to Duff-level recognition is a long one. Since I'm a celebrity in my own mind, I assumed that the rest of the free world would jump on board after my show aired. Six episodes were more than enough to make me an international superstar, right? No, as it turns out, not at all.

After *Downtown Girls* hit the airwaves, I did get recognized every so often, but not nearly as much or by as many studly hockey players as I'd hoped. And if I did, it would always be at the least-opportune times. Once, a naked lady tapped me on the shoulder in the gym locker room; another time, a guy started squealing with excitement while I was in Home Depot buying nails—wearing overalls. But at legitimate celebrity events and parties, no one said a word.

"People are definitely looking at you," my friend Dorit whispered at a U.S. Open party that summer. "But this is New York; no one just *goes up* to celebrities and starts gushing."

She was right; I've seen loads of A-listers roaming around Manhattan but I'd rather drunk dial my grandma than run up to them and coo about how awesome they are.

"Honestly though, I don't know why you care," she said. "Being famous and having people come up to you sounds awful. Anonymity is so much better!"

"The hell it is," I snorted into my drink.

I've been anonymous my whole life and it's only really useful when you're shoplifting or doing the walk of shame.

She and I were sitting in the VIP section of the party, right next to a bored-looking blond girl and her normal looking boyfriend. I was too busy scanning the crowd for hot guys to pay much attention to the small cluster of fans gathered at the velvet ropes.

"Hey, can we take a picture with you?"

A small, stocky gay guy was waving me over to the velvet ropes as his twin brother and a group of giggling girls held up cameras.

"See!" Dorit laughed. "People *do* know who you are! Yay!"

I smoothed my dress and strutted over. One of the girls mouthed, "I love your show," as the boys sidled next to me for a photo.

"I'm really sorry you fell," the gay one said.

Fell? In one episode I tripped a little bit, but that was hardly a standout moment in the series. What an odd thing to lead with. But still, people are weird, and it was my job, you know, as a very famous celebrity, to be gracious.

"Thank you," I said earnestly.

"I know, it was awful," said his non-gay brother. "But we're still *such* fans of yours. Go USA!"

"Um . . . yes," I said. Whichever celebrity they thought I was, it wasn't Shallon Lester. But we were already in photo position and I didn't have the heart to embarrass them—or myself. "Go USA," I cheered.

They gushed their thanks and I scooted back to my seat.

"I think they thought I was Lindsey Vonn," I told Dorit with a heavy sigh.

I sulked into my vodka soda until ten minutes later, when the group of fans returned.

"You're not Lindsey Vonn, are you?" said the gay guy fearfully. "Omigosh I am *so sorry!*"

He and his brother flooded me with apologies but the girls scratched their heads.

"Wait, you thought she was Lindsey Vonn?" a brunette asked.

"Yes!" hissed the gay in embarrassment. "Who did *you* think she was, smarty pants?"

"She's Shallon Lester, *duh!*"

I puffed with pride. At least one person on earth had seen the show and wasn't afraid to admit it.

"Yeah," said another girl, chiming in. "I mean, who the hell is Lindsey Vonn?"

"Excuse me," said a voice from behind me. It was the blond girl, who was now standing—towering, actually—over me. "But *I'm* Lindsey Vonn."

Psych

I could have easily titled this essay "The Worst $20 I've Ever Spent," because that perfectly sums up my experience with a psychic.

A week prior, my friend had seen a clairvoyant who had accurately deduced that she had once had a miscarriage, which we thought was a pretty risky and random assumption to throw out there. If she could deduce that, I felt certain that she could help me find the boyfriend I'd recently misplaced.

Luc was a professional poker player I had been dating for a few months, and we had just begun to fall in love. At least, that was *my* view of the situation. I had finally decided to really open my heart to him and dive in when he just . . . vanished. I hadn't heard from him since our last date, two weeks previously. I should have known better than to trust a man who deceives people for a living.

Our evening hadn't been anything out of the ordinary—no fights or spinach in the teeth or discoveries of giant condom stockpiles. Yet when I didn't hear from him the next day, something in the pit of my stomach told me it was over. My friends said I was being paranoid and ridiculous, that he was just busy. But the heart knows. *Maybe he's dead!* I thought hopefully, but Google told me he was very much alive, competing in a tournament up in Toronto.

I thought about throwing clothes and a passport into a plastic bag, walking to the train station, and heading north. I had the romantic notion to ride until the landscape became flat and verdant and the people looked tall and pale.

I could hide out at a ratty hotel like a criminal on the lam and eat gravy waffles alone in a diner, drifting after him, a shadow, looming like a cloud.

But I feared a land so full of hockey players might offer too many distractions, so instead of braving the Great White North, I turned to the mystical arts. I had no choice! I was in that half-breakup stage where my mind was consumed with obsessive thoughts. I needed respite, something to soothe my addled brain. And since I was out of Xanax, this seemed to be the next best thing.

The psychic my friend had seen was out of town, but as luck (or so it seemed at the time) would have it, a glimpse into the future was just a door away.

Above the pizza parlor next door to my apartment lived a middle-aged Puerto Rican woman whose window diplayed a neon sign advertising her psychic skills. I would often see her sitting in a lawn chair on the sidewalk, trying to entice people to come in for a reading while simultaneously hollering at her grubby grandchildren to stop playing in the garbage bags.

I probably should have looked around for a more reputable psychic, but after having checked my texts, e-mail, and Facebook 840 times that day hoping to hear from Luc, I realized beggars weren't about to be choosers.

I should note that I am a huge believer in the supernatural, clairvoyance, and mysticism in general. My grandmother gives eerily accurate tarot readings, while I'm pretty sure my mother can remember her past lives.

As for me, I can manipulate the future with powerful spell work. I'm particularly adept at binding and neutralization spells, which are basically preambles to a curse. Sometimes I would put a little too much zeal into the spell and it'd backfire into a full-on hex. But whatever, screw 'em.

The point is, I'm very well versed with magic and divination and I didn't go into this palm reading as a skeptic. But isn't it fair to assume that if this person could spend money on neon signs and Manhattan rent, she could maybe invest a little time and money in learning palmistry? Maybe even a cool $12.95 for a book on the subject?

False.

I had settled on a palm reading as opposed to voodoo because 1) it was cheap and I'd already blown $30 that day on magazines and candy, and 2) I had more lines on my hands than anyone I'd ever met. In sixth grade my friend Dorit nicknamed me Callisto, after one of Jupiter's heavily crevassed moons. (Nerd alert!)

I rang the bell and was buzzed into a dusty residential apartment building, where the psychic poked her head out of her door.

"Hello, hello," the rotund woman said warmly as she waddled into the hallway and motioned me in. "Welcome to the Lair of Mystery!"

The heady scent of roasting pork chops and fried food assaulted me immediately—not exactly the nectar of the gods, but delightful in its own way.

"You'll have to excuse me, I just made dinner for my grandchildren," she said as I stepped into the Lair of Meat, which was cleverly disguised as a shabby one-bedroom apartment littered with knickknacks and sticky-looking children watching TV.

"Uh, hi," I said awkwardly as the kids sniggered at me into their Mountain Dew.

She lumbered past me into the bedroom, where her white-haired husband was watching TV in his boxers.

"Henry! Out! I need the space." She shooed him and instructed me to have a seat on the grimy bedspread. "Now, I want you to think of two questions you want answered."

Is he the one? And *Will I be famous?* immediately sprang to mind.

Not exactly a peek into the mind of a Nobel laureate, but whatever. I am what I am.

For $20, she told me, I would receive an assessment of my past and present, as well as a "glimpse" into my future.

What was this, a psychic for friggin' amnesiacs? I *know* my past and my present.

But what the hey, I thought, *I'm already here and she could probably use the cash to buy her husband some pants; might as well give it a whirl.*

The true mystery of this lair was how she could pour out such crap with a straight face. Who was I kidding? She wasn't going to be able to tell me why Luc had disappeared, or whether I was doomed to a lifetime of heartbreak, or whether I would be able to stretch my fifteen minutes of fame into a full hour. She didn't even know where my heart or head or life line—or any other line—was. She just looked at my hands, furrowed her brow, and spouted vague nonsense.

"I see you like to help people."

True. Even sociopaths help people if it has some benefit for them.

"I see that you're concerned about the people you love."

If they give me candy/sex/money occasionally, and might per-haps give me more one day, then yes. True again.

"I see that you're going to be busy next year."

Ahh, her powers of divination told her that I am *not* of retire-ment age. Uncanny!

"What about my career?" I asked.

"Hmm, oooh, I see that you're not very motivated right now . . ."

Actually I had just started working on this book and was in the middle of filming *Downtown Girls*, so . . . false. I began paying more attention to the smell of pork chops than what was happening in the Lair of Malarkey.

"I see that you aren't where you want to be."

"Yep, that's for sure." I nodded dimly and sniffed the air like a dog. Where I wanted to be was in her kitchen, eating butter-laden mashed potatoes.

"I see that there was trauma in your life."

Duh. I didn't need a psychic to tell me that one. My eyes had now glassed over. Gravy, was I smelling gravy too? Eventually, I just gave up and turned my hands over to indicate I'd heard enough non-sense, but that didn't stop her from rambling on.

"Your chakras are blocked! But I can unblock them for you. I'll need to give you a crystal and meditate on this and light some candles . . . would you be interested in accepting my help?"

Some people think that the term "Gypsy" is derogatory, but that's because they've clearly never met one. Gypsies are indeed a shifty, deceitful bunch—all nomads are. There are just certain sectors of the population who are not to be trusted. Redheads, for example.

Maybe some Gypsies have "the gift," but the rest of them try to dupe people into elaborate and expensive "candle rituals" to cleanse their cloudy auras, which was clearly happening now in the Lair of Moneygrubbery.

I tore my thoughts away from warm biscuits sopping up gravy and giblets and politely declined the candle therapy.

"Fine," she snapped. "Twenty dollars."

I suppressed a sigh and tried to stand up, but something held me back. Something strong and powerful. Something unnatural . . .

"I see you have sat in gum."

Acknowledgments

Nothing worthwhile in my life would be possible without the following people:

Mama and Gigi, who have always made me feel like a success, even when I worked at a pest-control company. My best friends, Klo, Mars, Pfeiffy, and Holly, without whom I probably would've dated worse and eaten better. My NSLP, Hilary Lyle Mann, who I couldn't love more if I'd given birth to her. Dorit, Christine, Ellen, Sam, Shelby, and Nasim, who have known and tolerated me since before I started lying about my age. And to Meg Thompson at LJK Literary and Random House's Talia Krohn—thank you for encouraging and supporting me despite my shaky grammar and run-on sentences.

And of course, thank you to all of the boys who made these stories possible. I loved each one of you in my own frantic way. To those I left out, you can thank me later.

About the Author

Shallon Lester is the star of MTV's reality series *Downtown Girls* and coauthor of the teen novel *Hot Mess*. A twenty-first century Carrie Bradshaw (only with a better nose and cheaper shoes), Shallon has written for *Glamour* magazine, the *New York Daily News,* and *Gossip Girl.* She loves hockey and lip gloss and is fluent in French, Italian, and sexting. She lives in Manhattan, New York. You can find her on Twitter @DowntownShallon and keep up on her ongoing adventures at www.ShallonOnline.com.